My Home

Tips for Operating Your Home

Tom Feiza
Mr. Fix-It

Published by
Mr. Fix-It Press
N8 W28892 Shepherds Way
Waukesha, WI 53188

Phone: (262) 303-4884
Fax: (262) 303-4883
E-mail: Tom@misterfix-it.com
www.howtooperateyourhome.com
or www.htoyh.com

Notice:

This book is available at special discounts for bulk purchases, sales promotions, premiums, fund-raising, or educational use. For details, contact the publisher.

Second edition, 2013
ISBN: 978-0-9832018-4-7
Printed in the United States of America

Be Safe!

The information in this book has been carefully assembled to ensure that it is as accurate as possible. However, the book provides general information only, and it is sold with the understanding that the publisher and author are not rendering legal or professional services.

This book does not provide product-specific information, and you should consult the manufacturer of the product or equipment for specific information. Operation and maintenance information is provided for general understanding only.

When attempting a home repair project, always consult professionals and follow label directions. Companies that manufacture equipment and home repair products are the ultimate authorities. Follow their instructions.

Many home repair, operation, and maintenance projects involve a certain degree of risk and should be approached with care. You should only attempt repairs if you have read and understood the instructions for the product, equipment, or tool that you are using. If questions or problems arise, consult a professional or the manufacturer.

Due to the variability of local conditions, construction materials, and personal skills, neither the author nor the publisher assumes responsibility for any injuries suffered or for damages or other losses that may result from the information presented.

Acknowledgements

Special thanks go to all the people who listen to my radio show, watch my television appearances, attend my seminars, use my home inspection service, and read my newspaper column. Your questions, answers, and tips made this book possible. Many manufacturers have provided me with excellent technical information, and I value their help.

My editor, Leah Carson, took my rough copy and made the information much more useful and user-friendly. Lynn Eckstein designed my Mr. Fix-It logo years ago. Tom Feiza III created the cover and the wonderful interior layout.

Lindsay Mefford (Feiza) created the artwork for this revised edition from our originals and my rough sketches.

Most importantly, I owe a lot to my wife, Gayle, and our kids, Lindsay and Tom. They helped me keep things in proper perspective by dragging me out of the office for vacations and family time.

Please enjoy my book and have a great fix-it day!

Tom Feiza – "Mr. Fix-It"

Author . . . . .Tom Feiza, a.k.a. Mr. Fix-It
Editor . . . . .Leah Carson, Excellent Words, LLC (leah@excellentwords.com)
Artwork .Justin Racinowski, Lindsay Mefford, Tom Feiza
Layout/Cover Art .Tom Feiza III (tomfeiza@gmail.com)

Table of Contents

CHAPTER 1 – STRUCTURE, FRAMING 1

Foundation 1
Pier, Pile Foundations 1
Slab Foundations 2
Protecting Foundations 2
Protecting Full-Depth Foundations 3
Foundation Surface Drainage 3
Wood Framing 4
Wall Framing, Studs 4
Floor Support Systems 5
Roof Framing 5
Stucco 6
Brick Home 6

CHAPTER 2 – INSULATION & VENTILATION . . .7

Insulation Basics 7
Air Movement – Heat Loss 7
Typical Insulation 8
Ventilation – Types .8
Attic Ventilation 9
Bathroom Ventilation 9
Kitchen Ventilation 10
Heat Recovery Ventilator 10

CHAPTER 3 – DOORS, WINDOWS 11

Exterior Doors 11
Interior Doors 11
Door Adjustments .12
Overhead Garage Doors 12
Garage Door Operator 13
Windows 13
Window Parts 14
Window Glass or Glazing 14

CHAPTER 4 – ROOF 15

Roof Types 15
Roofs – General Terms 15
Asphalt Shingle Roof 16
Roof Materials 16
Tile, Slate 17
Roof Venting – Attic Venting 17
Flat, Low-Slope Roofs 18
Roof Gutters and Drainage 18
Roof Plumbing Vents 19
Bituminous Membranes 19

CHAPTER 5 – FIREPLACE, CHIMNEY 20

Masonry Chimney .20
Masonry Fireplace Parts 20
Masonry Chimney Parts 21
Metal Chimneys 21
Metal Prefabricated Fireplace 22
Direct Vent Fireplace 22

CHAPTER 6 – HEATING 23

Warm Air Furnace 23
Forced Air Heating Systems 23
Forced Air Distribution Systems 24
Heat Pump Systems 24
Filtering for Forced Air Heating 25
Air Filter Types 25
Air Filters – Higher Efficiency 26
Hydronic Heating System 26
Steam Heating Systems 27
Fuel Oil Heating Systems 27
Ductwork – Dampers 28
High and Low Returns – Cold Climates 28
Thermostat – Heating and Cooling 29
Digital Thermostat 29
Humidifier System and Controls 30
Heat System Disconnects 30

CHAPTER 7 – AIR CONDITIONING 31

Air Conditioning 31
Air Conditioning – Fan Unit Locations 31
Cooling – Heat Pump 32
Air Conditioning Leaks 32
Refrigeration Cycle 33
Air Conditioning Condenser Maintenance . . .33
Evaporative Cooler – Swamp Cooler 34
Evaporative Cooler Details 34

CHAPTER 8 – ENERGY 35

Natural Gas 35
Natural Gas Distribution, Valves 35
Fuel Oil 36
Propane 36
Electrical 37
Gas Shut-Off 37

CHAPTER 9 – PLUMBING 38
Water Supply – Municipal, Cold Climate 38
Water Supply – Municipal, Warm Climate 38
Water Supply – Private Well 39
Water Distribution with Basement – Cold Climate ..39
Water Distribution with Slab –Warm Climate 40
Water Distribution with Crawl Space 40
Drainage, Waste and Vent System 41
Septic System 41
Water Heater – Gas 42
Water Heater – Electric 42
Water Softener 43
Water Backflow Prevention 43
Typical Toilet 44
Shut-Off Valves – Appliances 44
Garbage Disposal 45
Hose Faucets 45
Pounding Pipes 46
Sanitary and Storm Sewers 46
Sanitary Pumps 47
Plugged Drains 47

CHAPTER 10 – ELECTRICITY 48
Electrical – Overhead Feed 48
Electrical – Underground Feed 48
Electrical Main Panel 49
Electrical Main Panel – Warm, Dry Climate 49
Ground Fault Circuit Interrupters (GFCI) 50
Polarity 50
Outlets, Cords and Plugs 51
Circuit Breaker Resets 51

CHAPTER 11 – SAFETY 52
Carbon Monoxide 52
Fire Safety 52
Lead, Asbestos, Radon, Mold 53
Electrical 53

CHAPTER 12 – SERVICE REQUIREMENTS 54
Service Requirements by the Calendar 54
Daily and Weekly 54
Monthly 55
Spring 55
Summer 56
Fall 57
Winter 58
Periodic Maintenance and Service as Needed 58

ORDERING INFORMATION 59

Chapter 1 – Structure, Framing

Foundation

1. Foundation types vary with local weather and soil conditions.

2. In cold climates, the foundation must extend below the frost line, and this often results in the decision to build a full-depth basement.

3. In moderate climates, crawl spaces are common.

4. In warm climates, slab on grade foundations are common.

5. The foundation supports the structure of the home and separates the home from the soil.

6. All foundations must be protected from water.

7. Never allow water to collect near the foundation.

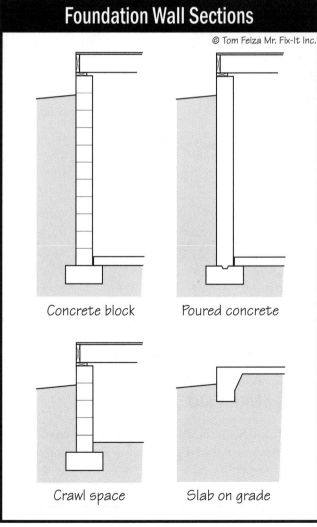

Foundation Wall Sections

© Tom Feiza Mr. Fix-It Inc.

Concrete block   Poured concrete

Crawl space   Slab on grade

S004

Pier, Pile Foundations

1. With soft or poor soil conditions, the foundation is often extended to solid soil or rock with a pier or pile providing support.

2. Piles are driven into the soil, and piers are poured in a drilled hole.

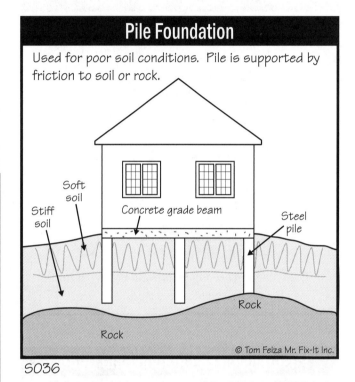

Pile Foundation

Used for poor soil conditions. Pile is supported by friction to soil or rock.

Soft soil

Stiff soil

Concrete grade beam

Steel pile

Rock

Rock

© Tom Feiza Mr. Fix-It Inc.

S036

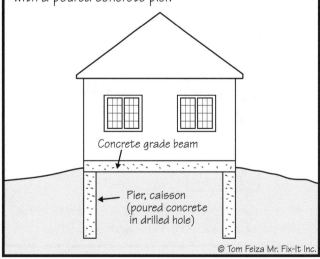

Pier, Caisson Foundation

Used for poor soil conditions. Drilled hole is filled with a poured concrete pier.

Concrete grade beam

Pier, caisson (poured concrete in drilled hole)

© Tom Feiza Mr. Fix-It Inc.

S037

Slab Foundations

1. A slab foundation floats on the soil and must remain uniform and rigid.

2. With newer construction, a slab is often reinforced with steel cables stretched inside tubes to make the slab rigid.

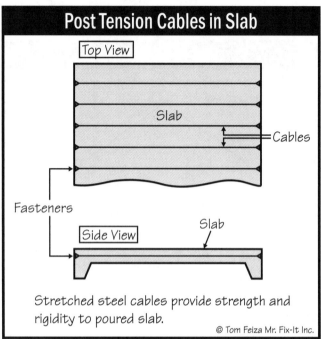

Post Tension Cables in Slab

Top View

Slab

Cables

Fasteners

Side View — Slab

Stretched steel cables provide strength and rigidity to poured slab.

© Tom Feiza Mr. Fix-It Inc.

S034

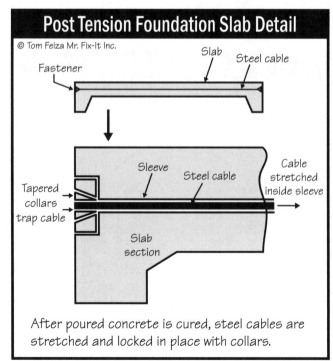

Post Tension Foundation Slab Detail

© Tom Feiza Mr. Fix-It Inc.

Fastener

Slab

Steel cable

Sleeve

Steel cable

Cable stretched inside sleeve

Tapered collars trap cable

Slab section

After poured concrete is cured, steel cables are stretched and locked in place with collars.

S035

Protecting Foundations

1. All types of foundations – slabs, crawl spaces and full-depth foundations – must be protected from water.

2. Surface grading, gutters and downspouts should direct water away from the foundation.

3. Water next to a foundation can cause leaks and structural movement.

4. Water next to a foundation can cause heaving with frost and can push vertical walls inward.

5. Lack of water near a foundation can cause settling.

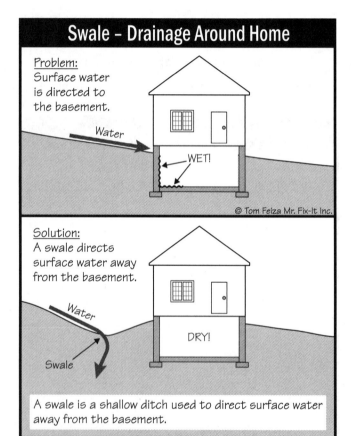

Swale – Drainage Around Home

Problem:
Surface water is directed to the basement.

Water

WET!

© Tom Feiza Mr. Fix-It Inc.

Solution:
A swale directs surface water away from the basement.

Water

DRY!

Swale

A swale is a shallow ditch used to direct surface water away from the basement.

S015

Must Know – Must Do

1. Know your local soil and foundation conditions, and always protect your foundation by controlling water.

Protecting Full-Depth Foundations

1. Often a full-depth foundation is protected from water by a drain tile and sump pump system.

2. The drain tile collects water from around the foundation and routes it to a sump pump.

3. The sump pump ejects water to the surface or to a storm sewer system.

4. Block walls in a basement are also protected with a mortar and tar coating or a special drainage plane.

5. Tile consists of perforated plastic pipe or spaced concrete tubes.

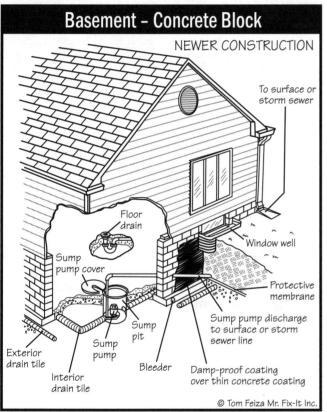

Basement - Concrete Block

NEWER CONSTRUCTION

To surface or storm sewer

Floor drain

Window well

Sump pump cover

Protective membrane

Sump pit

Sump pump discharge to surface or storm sewer line

Exterior drain tile

Sump pump

Bleeder

Damp-proof coating over thin concrete coating

Interior drain tile

© Tom Feiza Mr. Fix-It Inc.

B005

Must Know – Must Do

1. Understand your home's foundation and construction.

2. Keep water away from the foundation with proper grading, gutters and downspout extensions.

Foundation Surface Drainage

1. The soil around the foundation should start six inches below the wood structure to prevent moisture and pest damage.

2. The soil around a foundation should slope away from the foundation to move water away.

3. Check drainage in hidden areas, such as under decks.

4. Exterior concrete must slope away from the foundation.

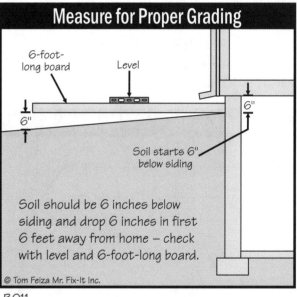

Measure for Proper Grading

6-foot-long board

Level

6"

6"

Soil starts 6" below siding

Soil should be 6 inches below siding and drop 6 inches in first 6 feet away from home – check with level and 6-foot-long board.

© Tom Feiza Mr. Fix-It Inc.

B011

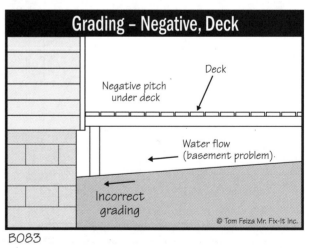

Grading - Negative, Deck

Deck

Negative pitch under deck

Water flow (basement problem)

Incorrect grading

© Tom Feiza Mr. Fix-It Inc.

B083

Must Know – Must Do

1. Always keep soil and water away from the foundation and wood framing.

Wood Framing

1. Most homes in the U.S. are built with a wood frame.

2. Some older homes will have solid brick or solid masonry walls.

3. A few homes are built with a solid log frame.

4. Today, wood frame homes are built with a platform method in which one level is built at a time.

5. When longer lumber was available, homes were built with a balloon frame.

6. The wood framing must be placed on a solid foundation protected from water and soil.

7. The framing is covered with house wrap, siding and flashings to protect it from water.

8. The framing is filled with insulation to limit heat loss and gain.

Wall Framing, Studs

1. Most homes are framed with 2 by 4 or 2 by 6 wood studs.

2. Some older homes, and homes in areas with termites, may be framed with masonry.

3. Wood framing allows for insulation and for electrical and plumbing runs.

4. At door and window openings in the framing, headers support the structure above.

5. A modern "brick" home has a wood frame and a brick veneer or covering.

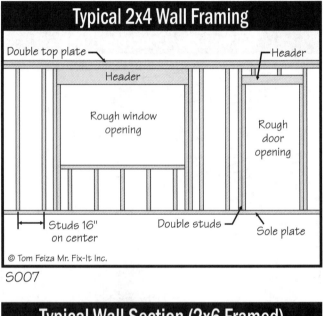

Typical 2x4 Wall Framing

© Tom Feiza Mr. Fix-It Inc.

S007

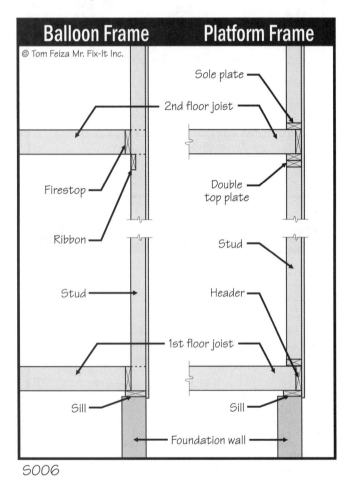

S006

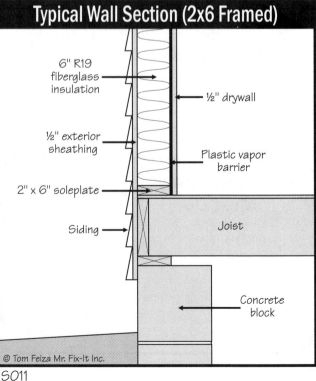

S011

4

Floor Support Systems

1. Floor joists support the subfloor in the home and are normally spaced every 16 inches.

2. The floor joists extend from exterior walls to interior load-bearing walls.

3. Floor joists often consist of solid lumber. Dimensions vary with the span and spacing.

4. Newer homes may have a manufactured "I" joist or a "TJI" joist that can span a greater distance.

5. Floor trusses are used to span a long distance without interior wall support.

6. Never cut or modify the floor framing without professional advice.

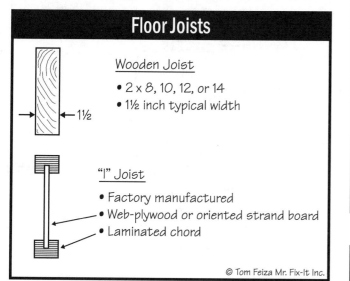

Floor Joists

Wooden Joist
- 2 x 8, 10, 12, or 14
- 1½ inch typical width

— 1½

"I" Joist
- Factory manufactured
- Web-plywood or oriented strand board
- Laminated chord

© Tom Feiza Mr. Fix-It Inc.

S040

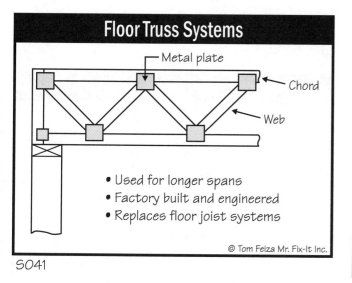

Floor Truss Systems

Metal plate

Chord

Web

- Used for longer spans
- Factory built and engineered
- Replaces floor joist systems

© Tom Feiza Mr. Fix-It Inc.

S041

Roof Framing

1. Roofs are often framed with wood joists and covered with a plywood or OSB (oriented strand board) deck to support shingles.

2. In modern construction, roofs are often framed with a 2 by 4 truss system for greater spans using less material.

3. With exposed cathedral ceilings or log home construction, a ridge beam may support the roof structure joist framing.

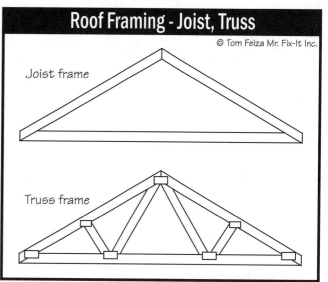

Roof Framing - Joist, Truss

© Tom Feiza Mr. Fix-It Inc.

Joist frame

Truss frame

S014

Roof Rafter Span - Ridge Beam

© Tom Feiza Mr. Fix-It Inc.

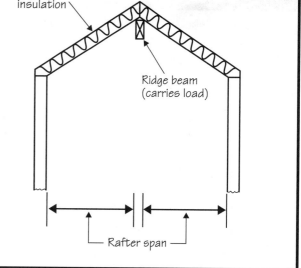

Rafters with insulation

Ridge beam (carries load)

Rafter span

S025

Stucco

1. Traditional stucco has been used for many years as an exterior cladding system. It consists of three coats of a cement material over block, wood lath or wire mesh.

2. In recent years, synthetic stucco has become popular. This is a coating placed over rigid foam insulation board.

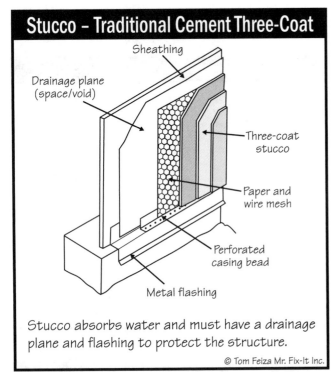

Stucco – Traditional Cement Three-Coat

- Sheathing
- Drainage plane (space/void)
- Three-coat stucco
- Paper and wire mesh
- Perforated casing bead
- Metal flashing

Stucco absorbs water and must have a drainage plane and flashing to protect the structure.

© Tom Feiza Mr. Fix-It Inc.

X014

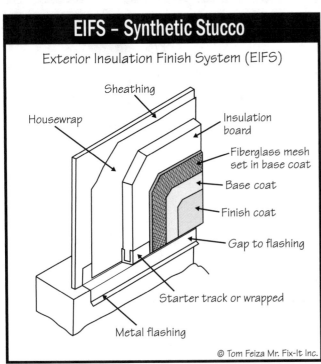

EIFS – Synthetic Stucco

Exterior Insulation Finish System (EIFS)

- Housewrap
- Sheathing
- Insulation board
- Fiberglass mesh set in base coat
- Base coat
- Finish coat
- Gap to flashing
- Starter track or wrapped
- Metal flashing

© Tom Feiza Mr. Fix-It Inc.

X015

Brick Home

1. Most "brick" homes built since 1900 are really wood-framed structures with a brick veneer.

2. The brick veneer is placed outside the wood frame and is supported by the masonry foundation.

3. Prior to 1900, some homes were built with solid brick walls that incorporated several layers of brick.

4. Brick veneer should have small weep holes at the base of the wall to drain water that may enter the wall.

5. At the base of the wall, there should also be flashing to direct water to the outside.

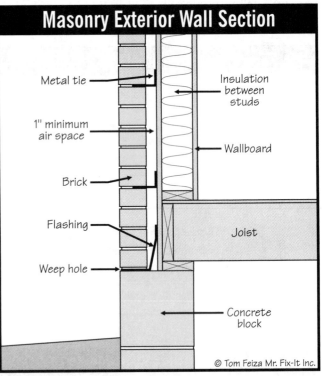

Masonry Exterior Wall Section

- Metal tie
- 1" minimum air space
- Brick
- Flashing
- Weep hole
- Insulation between studs
- Wallboard
- Joist
- Concrete block

© Tom Feiza Mr. Fix-It Inc.

S005

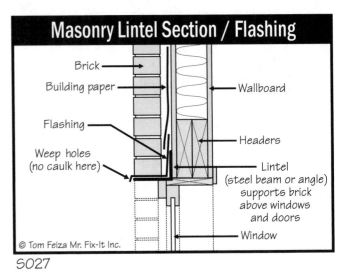

Masonry Lintel Section / Flashing

- Brick
- Building paper
- Flashing
- Weep holes (no caulk here)
- Wallboard
- Headers
- Lintel (steel beam or angle) supports brick above windows and doors
- Window

© Tom Feiza Mr. Fix-It Inc.

S027

Chapter 2 – Insulation & Ventilation

Insulation Basics

1. Insulation in a modern home consists of fiberglass, cellulose, mineral wood, foam, or a combination of these materials.

2. Insulation must completely surround the heated spaces.

3. In modern construction, a vapor retarder is placed between insulation and the heated space to stop the flow of air and moisture.

4. Insulation materials reduce air movement and heat flow.

5. The effectiveness of insulation is measured in R-value.

6. The higher the R-value, the higher the resistance to heat flow.

7. Insulation requirements are based on climate conditions.

8. In northern climates, typical attic-to-ceiling insulation is R-38, or about 12 inches of insulation.

9. Insulation must provide a continuous blanket to be effective.

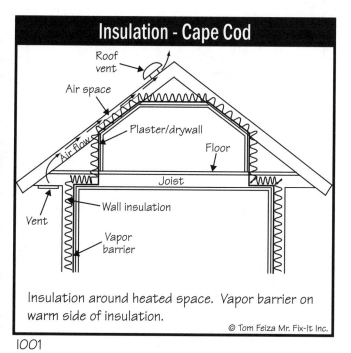

Insulation - Cape Cod

Insulation around heated space. Vapor barrier on warm side of insulation.

© Tom Feiza Mr. Fix-It Inc.

1001

Air Movement – Heat Loss

1. Air leaks and air movement allow significant heat loss and moisture movement – a bad thing.

2. All air leaks from the heated space into the attic must be avoided.

3. Lack of insulation allows for a convective air loop and accelerated transfer of energy.

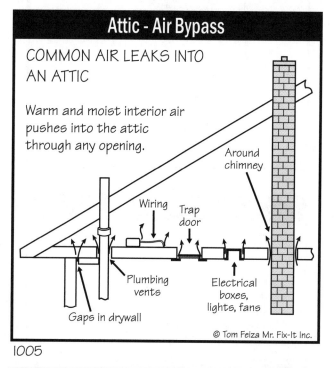

Attic - Air Bypass

COMMON AIR LEAKS INTO AN ATTIC

Warm and moist interior air pushes into the attic through any opening.

© Tom Feiza Mr. Fix-It Inc.

1005

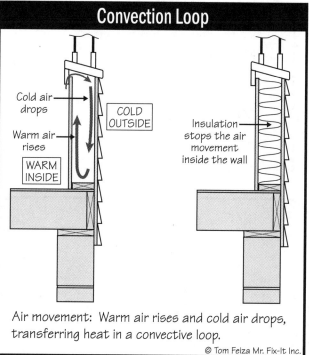

Convection Loop

Air movement: Warm air rises and cold air drops, transferring heat in a convective loop.

© Tom Feiza Mr. Fix-It Inc.

1007

Typical Insulation

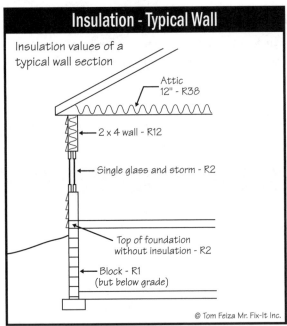

Insulation - Typical Wall

Insulation values of a typical wall section

Attic 12" - R38

2 x 4 wall - R12

Single glass and storm - R2

Top of foundation without insulation - R2

Block - R1 (but below grade)

© Tom Feiza Mr. Fix-It Inc.

I020

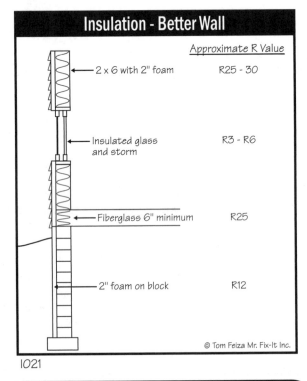

Insulation - Better Wall

	Approximate R Value
2 x 6 with 2" foam	R25 - 30
Insulated glass and storm	R3 - R6
Fiberglass 6" minimum	R25
2" foam on block	R12

© Tom Feiza Mr. Fix-It Inc.

I021

> ### Must Know – Must Do
>
> 1. Be aware of the construction of your home and how you might improve energy efficiency with more effective insulation materials and air sealing.

Ventilation – Types

1. Ventilation is confusing.

2. One type of ventilation refers to the removal of moisture or contaminates. This is point (source) ventilation.

3. Ventilation also refers to general ventilation of the attic or crawl space.

4. Attic ventilation vents heat to the outside and removes moisture.

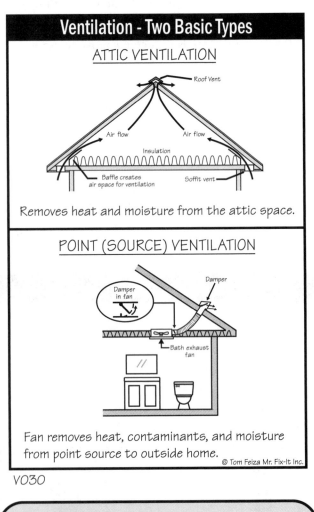

Ventilation - Two Basic Types

ATTIC VENTILATION

Roof Vent

Air flow   Air flow

Insulation

Baffle creates air space for ventilation   Soffit vent

Removes heat and moisture from the attic space.

POINT (SOURCE) VENTILATION

Damper in fan   Damper

Bath exhaust fan

Fan removes heat, contaminants, and moisture from point source to outside home.

© Tom Feiza Mr. Fix-It Inc.

V030

> ### Must Know – Must Do
>
> 1. Never allow excessive moisture to build up inside your home or crawl space.
>
> 2. Reduce the moisture in your home if you see condensation on the inside of windows.
>
> 3. In warm, humid conditions, consider running the air conditioner to remove excessive interior moisture.

Attic Ventilation

1. Attic ventilation appears simple – and it is, if it works properly.

2. Proper attic ventilation reduces heat buildup and removes moisture.

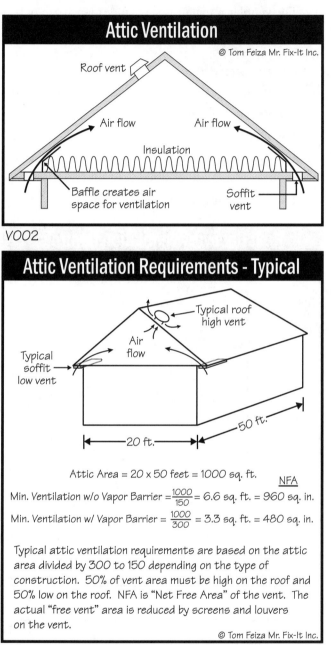

Attic Ventilation

© Tom Feiza Mr. Fix-It Inc.

Roof vent

Air flow   Air flow

Insulation

Baffle creates air space for ventilation

Soffit vent

V002

Attic Ventilation Requirements - Typical

Typical roof high vent

Air flow

Typical soffit low vent

50 ft.

20 ft.

Attic Area = 20 x 50 feet = 1000 sq. ft.

Min. Ventilation w/o Vapor Barrier = $\frac{1000}{150}$ = 6.6 sq. ft. = 960 sq. in.

Min. Ventilation w/ Vapor Barrier = $\frac{1000}{300}$ = 3.3 sq. ft. = 480 sq. in.

NFA

Typical attic ventilation requirements are based on the attic area divided by 300 to 150 depending on the type of construction. 50% of vent area must be high on the roof and 50% low on the roof. NFA is "Net Free Area" of the vent. The actual "free vent" area is reduced by screens and louvers on the vent.

© Tom Feiza Mr. Fix-It Inc.

V042

💡 **Must Know – Must Do**

1. Understand your attic ventilation, and never allow moisture to build up in an attic.

Bathroom Ventilation

1. Every bathroom with a shower should have an exhaust fan to remove excessive moisture.

2. All bathroom exhaust fans should be ducted through the roof or through an outside wall.

3. Dampers on bath fans and ducts must operate freely.

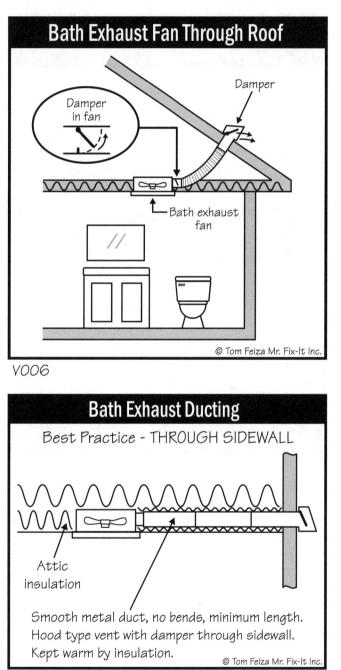

Bath Exhaust Fan Through Roof

Damper

Damper in fan

Bath exhaust fan

© Tom Feiza Mr. Fix-It Inc.

V006

Bath Exhaust Ducting

Best Practice - THROUGH SIDEWALL

Attic insulation

Smooth metal duct, no bends, minimum length. Hood type vent with damper through sidewall. Kept warm by insulation.

© Tom Feiza Mr. Fix-It Inc.

V018

Kitchen Ventilation

1. All kitchen cooking ranges should be vented to the outside to remove odors, heat and moisture.

2. The vent may be through the roof or through an outside wall.

3. Fans and filters must be cleaned on a routine basis.

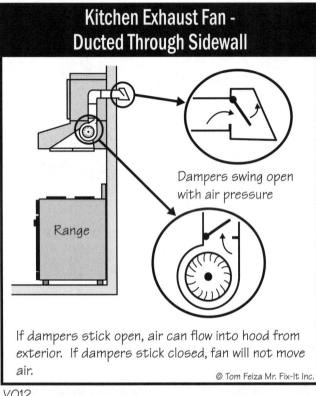

Kitchen Exhaust Fan - Ducted Through Sidewall

Dampers swing open with air pressure

Range

If dampers stick open, air can flow into hood from exterior. If dampers stick closed, fan will not move air.

© Tom Feiza Mr. Fix-It Inc.

V012

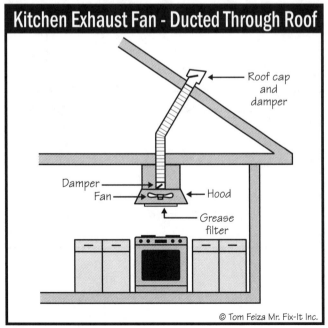

Kitchen Exhaust Fan - Ducted Through Roof

Roof cap and damper

Damper
Fan
Hood
Grease filter

© Tom Feiza Mr. Fix-It Inc.

V013

Heat Recovery Ventilator

1. Newer homes are very tight; there is a limited exchange of air with the outside.

2. Some newer homes are equipped with a heat recovery ventilation system.

3. The ventilator exhausts stale, moist air to the outside and captures heat from this exhaust air.

4. Heat is transferred to fresh air drawn from the outside and provided to the home.

5. The fresh air is often ducted into the return system of a forced air furnace.

6. The unit normally has two small fans and air filters.

7. The unit may operate manually; on a program; or according to interior humidity or total run time.

8. The unit requires maintenance of filters.

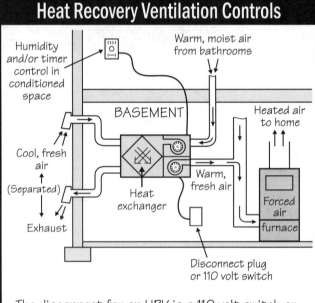

Heat Recovery Ventilation Controls

Humidity and/or timer control in conditioned space

Warm, moist air from bathrooms

BASEMENT

Heated air to home

Cool, fresh air

(Separated)

Exhaust

Heat exchanger

Warm, fresh air

Forced air furnace

Disconnect plug or 110 volt switch

The disconnect for an HRV is a 110 volt switch or plug. The control may be a combination of a timer and/or a humidistat.

© Tom Feiza Mr. Fix-It Inc.

V053

Must Know – Must Do

1. Understand the specific controls for your unit, and check for proper indoor humidity levels.

2. Maintain the filters.

Chapter 3 – Doors, Windows

Exterior Doors

1. Exterior doors are made in many styles. Most are constructed of wood, steel or fiberglass.

2. Wood-panel doors are constructed with floating panels to allow for the wood's expansion and contraction.

3. Metal and fiberglass doors have solid exterior surfaces and often have interior insulation.

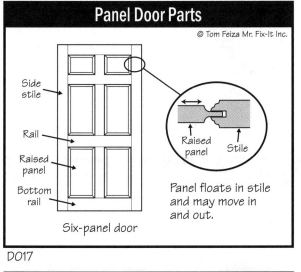

Panel Door Parts

© Tom Feiza Mr. Fix-It Inc.

Side stile
Rail
Raised panel
Bottom rail

Raised panel · Stile

Six-panel door

Panel floats in stile and may move in and out.

D017

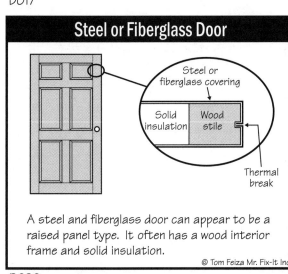

Steel or Fiberglass Door

Steel or fiberglass covering

Solid insulation · Wood stile

Thermal break

A steel and fiberglass door can appear to be a raised panel type. It often has a wood interior frame and solid insulation.

© Tom Feiza Mr. Fix-It Inc.

D020

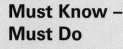

Must Know – Must Do

1. Maintain the finish and weatherstripping on all exterior doors.

2. Adjustments can be made to locksets and hinges if needed.

Interior Doors

1. Many variations exist for interior door styles and construction.

2. Many doors are six-panel, solid core or hollow core.

3. Doors may also be metal, composite, or wood veneer.

4. For closets, you may also find sliding, bypass or bi-fold doors.

5. Locksets for doors also vary for the type of application.

6. Exterior locksets may be knob-in-key. Bathrooms often have a simple lock with an exterior release in the doorknob.

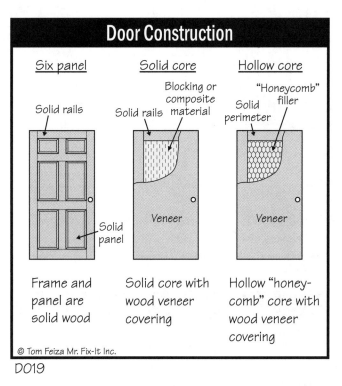

Door Construction

Six panel	Solid core	Hollow core
Solid rails	Blocking or composite material / Solid rails	"Honeycomb" filler / Solid perimeter
Solid panel	Veneer	Veneer
Frame and panel are solid wood	Solid core with wood veneer covering	Hollow "honeycomb" core with wood veneer covering

© Tom Feiza Mr. Fix-It Inc.

D019

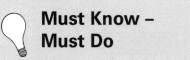

Must Know – Must Do

1. Lubricate hinges with a few drops of light oil yearly.

2. Doors, hinges and locksets can be adjusted as needed.

Door Adjustments

1. Folding and bypass doors allow numerous adjustments to raise, lower and tip the doors for proper fit.

2. Most door fit problems are due to loose or bent hardware.

3. Adjustments are simple to make but often difficult to understand.

Bypass / Sliding Door Adjustment #1

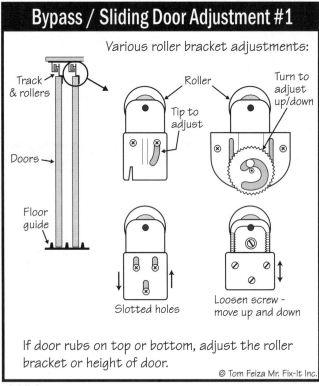

Various roller bracket adjustments:

Track & rollers

Roller

Turn to adjust up/down

Tip to adjust

Doors

Floor guide

Slotted holes

Loosen screw - move up and down

If door rubs on top or bottom, adjust the roller bracket or height of door.

© Tom Feiza Mr. Fix-It Inc.

D030

Bifold Door Tips

© Tom Feiza Mr. Fix-It Inc.

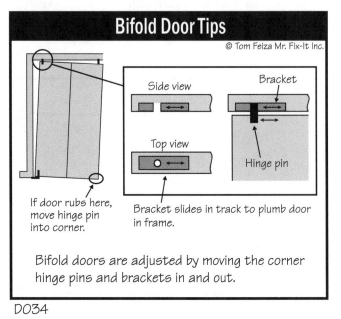

Side view

Bracket

Top view

Hinge pin

If door rubs here, move hinge pin into corner.

Bracket slides in track to plumb door in frame.

Bifold doors are adjusted by moving the corner hinge pins and brackets in and out.

D034

Overhead Garage Doors

1. An overhead garage door is the largest and heaviest moving part in your home.

2. The garage door can be dangerous. Never make adjustments or repairs unless you fully understand the operation of the door and door operator.

3. Overhead doors are lifted and balanced with a large extension or torsion spring.

4. The spring should be adjusted so the door can be lifted and operated with a few pounds of force.

5. The door should balance in the center of its travel.

6. All surfaces of a garage door should be painted – all six sides of the panels.

7. The rollers and tracks should be lubricated with garage door lubricant.

8. The hardware should be tightened on a routine basis.

Garage Door – Extension Spring Safety Cable

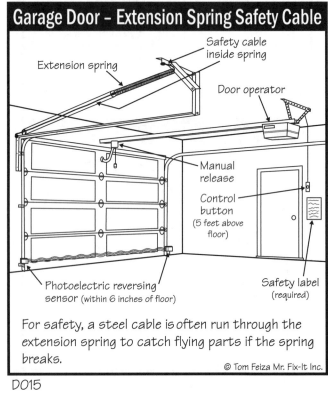

Safety cable inside spring

Extension spring

Door operator

Manual release

Control button (5 feet above floor)

Photoelectric reversing sensor (within 6 inches of floor)

Safety label (required)

For safety, a steel cable is often run through the extension spring to catch flying parts if the spring breaks.

© Tom Feiza Mr. Fix-It Inc.

D015

Must Know – Must Do

1. Maintain the rollers and hardware on a routine basis.

2. Have a professional adjust the spring.

Garage Door Operator

1. The garage door and its operator mechanism can be dangerous if not maintained and operated properly.

2. Refer to your door's operating manual for specific safety precautions.

3. The garage door, springs and hardware must be maintained to keep the garage door operator functioning properly.

4. Modern garage door operators have a photo-eye sensor to reverse the door if there is any obstruction below the door.

5. Older doors have a pressure-sensitive reverse – if the door hits something, it will reverse.

6. Garage doors and operators should be maintained per the manufacturer's requirements, and the safety reverse should be tested on a routine basis.

7. The operator button should be at least five feet from the floor to prevent children from playing with the door.

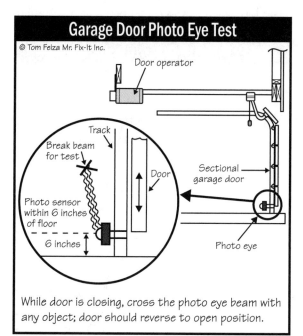

Garage Door Photo Eye Test

© Tom Feiza Mr. Fix-It Inc.

While door is closing, cross the photo eye beam with any object; door should reverse to open position.

D013

Must Know – Must Do

1. Have a professional adjust and test the garage door and operator on a routine basis.

2. Never allow children to operate or play with the door.

Windows

1. There are many types and styles of windows and window glass.

2. Windows are constructed of various materials, including wood, vinyl, composite, metal, and aluminum.

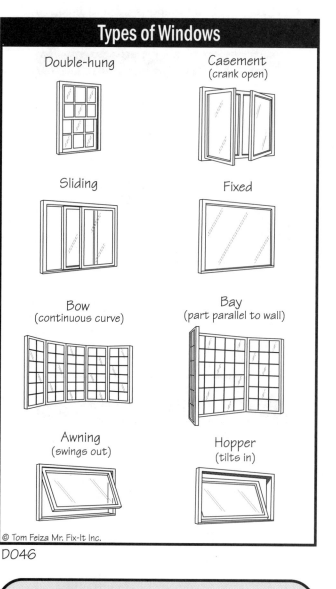

Types of Windows

Double-hung
Casement (crank open)
Sliding
Fixed
Bow (continuous curve)
Bay (part parallel to wall)
Awning (swings out)
Hopper (tilts in)

© Tom Feiza Mr. Fix-It Inc.

D046

Must Know – Must Do

1. Window finishes must be maintained to extend the life of the window.

2. Broken glass, broken springs, missing sash cords, and damaged hardware can present safety hazards – so be careful, and maintain the windows.

Window Parts

1. All windows must be maintained, adjusted and painted as needed.

2. Windows have a sill, drip and flashing to keep water outside your home.

3. Older, double-hung windows use a sash cord and weight to balance the weight of the window sash.

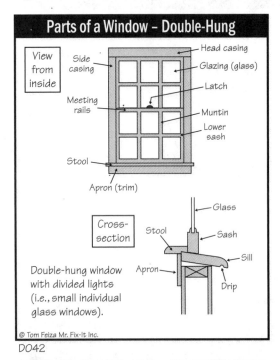

Parts of a Window – Double-Hung

View from inside

Side casing
Head casing
Glazing (glass)
Latch
Meeting rails
Muntin
Lower sash
Stool
Apron (trim)

Cross-section
Glass
Stool
Sash
Apron
Sill
Drip

Double-hung window with divided lights (i.e., small individual glass windows).

© Tom Feiza Mr. Fix-It Inc.
D042

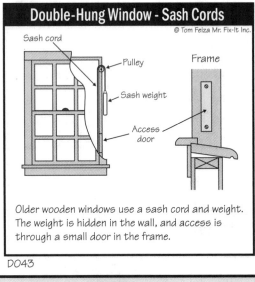

Double-Hung Window - Sash Cords

© Tom Feiza Mr. Fix-It Inc.

Sash cord
Pulley
Frame
Sash weight
Access door

Older wooden windows use a sash cord and weight. The weight is hidden in the wall, and access is through a small door in the frame.

D043

Must Know – Must Do

1. Understand the types of windows in your home, and carefully maintain them.

Window Glass or Glazing

1. Window glass (glazing) has become more efficient with modern technology.

2. Older windows often had a single pane of glass with an insulation or R-value of about 1.

3. In northern climates, window glazing often consists of multiple layers of glass, coatings, and special gas. R-values can be over R-4.

4. Windows with higher R-values limit heat transfer and make you feel more comfortable because less heat radiates through the glass to your body.

5. Special coatings on modern glass limit the movement of ultraviolet light through the glass. This reduces interior heat from sunlight and protects interior finishes from sun damage.

6. Storm windows increase the R-value.

7. A "foggy" insulated glass panel indicates that the seal between the glass panels has failed.

8. Failed insulated glass panels will not leak water or waste lots of energy, but the fog can't be cleaned.

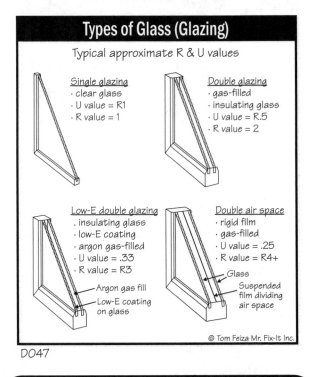

Types of Glass (Glazing)

Typical approximate R & U values

Single glazing
· clear glass
· U value = R1
· R value = 1

Double glazing
· gas-filled
· insulating glass
· U value = R.5
· R value = 2

Low-E double glazing
· insulating glass
· low-E coating
· argon gas-filled
· U value = .33
· R value = R3

Argon gas fill
Low-E coating on glass

Double air space
· rigid film
· gas-filled
· U value = .25
· R value = R4+

Glass
Suspended film dividing air space

© Tom Feiza Mr. Fix-It Inc.
D047

Must Know – Must Do

1. Understand your window type. Maintain finishes and weatherstripping.

Roof Types

1. Roofs keep a home watertight. They are designed for local weather conditions.
2. There are many roof shapes. Some are described below.
3. The slope of a roof refers to its angle or the rise over the horizontal run.
4. Roofs with a steep slope are more effective in shedding water.

Roofs – General Terms

1. Understand the basic components of your roof.
2. A valley is the intersection of two adjacent roof planes and may consist of metal or shingle materials.
3. A roof vent or ridge vent allows for ventilation of the roof by releasing hot air and moisture.
4. The ridge is the peak or top edge of the roof.
5. The eave is the overhang, soffit and fascia.
6. The rake is the extended overhang.
7. Plumbing vents appear as large open pipes penetrating the roof.
8. A chimney has metal flashing where the brick meets the roofing material.

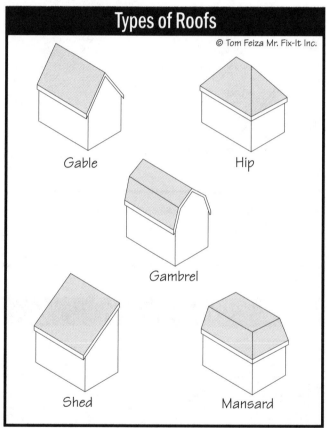

Types of Roofs

© Tom Feiza Mr. Fix-It Inc.

Gable

Hip

Gambrel

Shed

Mansard

R003

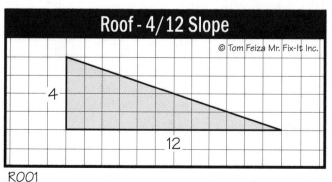

Roof - 4/12 Slope

© Tom Feiza Mr. Fix-It Inc.

4

12

R001

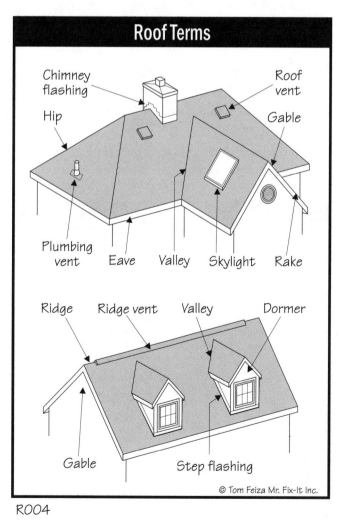

Roof Terms

Chimney flashing

Roof vent

Hip

Gable

Plumbing vent

Eave

Valley

Skylight

Rake

Ridge

Ridge vent

Valley

Dormer

Gable

Step flashing

© Tom Feiza Mr. Fix-It Inc.

R004

Asphalt Shingle Roof

1. Asphalt shingles are a very common roofing material.

2. Asphalt shingles consist of a fiberglass or fiber mat impregnated with asphalt and covered with granules.

3. The granules protect the asphalt from the sun.

4. Asphalt shingles can only be used on a roof with a 4/12 or greater slope unless there are special installation details.

5. Shingles are laid over roof felt covering a wood roof deck.

6. Nails fastening the shingle must penetrate the deck 3/4 inch or fully through the deck.

7. Metal flashings are often used at the rake edge and the drip edge.

8. A "three tab" shingle is shown here. It has distinctive cuts in the shingle, forming shingle tabs.

9. Newer asphalt shingles are often laminated or are an architectural style without tabs.

10. An asphalt shingle roof must be ventilated to keep the attic space dry and cool.

11. Excessive heat in the attic will shorten the life of the roof assembly.

12. Flashings must be used at all penetrations or connections to the roof.

Roof Materials

1. Wood shingles are smooth and flat, and they shed water.

2. Wood shakes are rough. They utilize a roofing felt to make the assembly shed water.

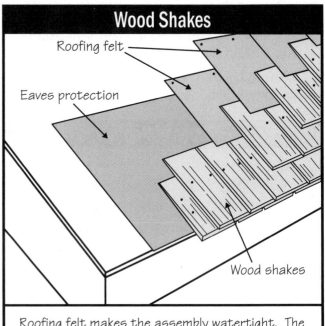

Wood Shakes

Roofing felt
Eaves protection
Wood shakes

© Tom Feiza Mr. Fix-It Inc.

Roofing felt makes the assembly watertight. The wood shakes shed most water and protect the roofing felt from sunlight.

R017

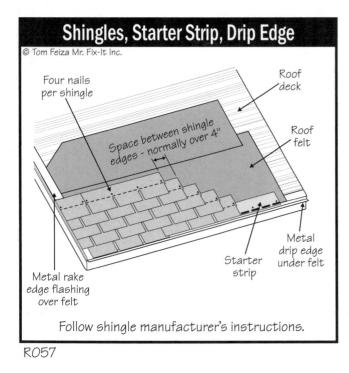

Shingles, Starter Strip, Drip Edge

© Tom Feiza Mr. Fix-It Inc.

Four nails per shingle
Roof deck
Space between shingle edges - normally over 4"
Roof felt
Metal drip edge under felt
Starter strip
Metal rake edge flashing over felt

Follow shingle manufacturer's instructions.

R057

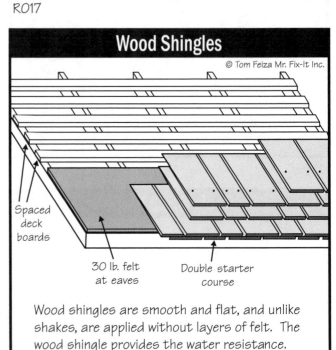

Wood Shingles

© Tom Feiza Mr. Fix-It Inc.

Spaced deck boards
30 lb. felt at eaves
Double starter course

Wood shingles are smooth and flat, and unlike shakes, are applied without layers of felt. The wood shingle provides the water resistance.

R020

Tile, Slate

1. Tile roofs are often used in warm climates because they are not damaged by the sun the way asphalt shingles are.

2. Tile roofs are often made of clay tile material, but they can also be cement or even coated metal.

3. Tiles are held in place with nails driven into wooden strips. The nails are hidden by the upper tile.

4. A roof felt under the tile helps keep the roof system water resistant.

5. Slate roofs consist of various natural stone materials and are flat like asphalt shingle roofs.

6. Slate is held in place with nails; roofing paper makes the assembly water resistant.

7. Both tile and slate roofs are slippery and fragile. Don't walk on a tile or slate roof.

8. Both tile and slate roofs offer very long life with limited maintenance.

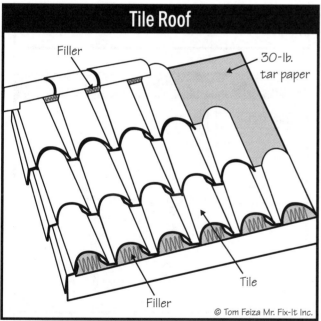

Tile Roof

Filler

30-lb. tar paper

Tile

Filler

© Tom Feiza Mr. Fix-It Inc.

R018

Must Know – Must Do

1. Know your type of roofing material.

2. Have tile and slate roofs checked by a professional every few years.

Roof Venting – Attic Venting

1. Roofs and attics are vented to remove excessive heat, protect the shingles, and stop heat transfer to the living space.

2. Heat can build up in the attic because of sunlight and the flow of heat from living spaces.

3. Keeping the roof cooler and the roof deck dry extends the life of the roofing material.

4. Static roof venting is often accomplished with a combination of vents in the overhangs and roof vents or ridge vents high on the roof.

5. Venting can also be accomplished with a roof exhaust fan and vents low on the roof.

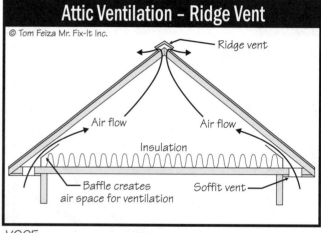

Attic Ventilation – Ridge Vent

© Tom Feiza Mr. Fix-It Inc.

Ridge vent

Air flow

Air flow

Insulation

Baffle creates air space for ventilation

Soffit vent

V005

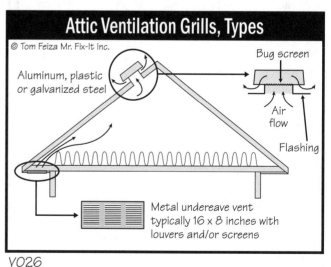

Attic Ventilation Grills, Types

© Tom Feiza Mr. Fix-It Inc.

Aluminum, plastic or galvanized steel

Bug screen

Air flow

Flashing

Metal undereave vent typically 16 x 8 inches with louvers and/or screens

V026

Flat, Low-Slope Roofs

1. Flat or low-slope roofs require a membrane type of roof – rubber, vinyl or similar material.

2. A flat or low-slope roof needs some pitch to move water to the edge or to a roof drain.

3. A common roofing material is rubber or EPDM, a single-ply membrane.

4. Usually, rubber roofs are fully adhered to a special base board.

5. Rubber roofs are fastened with a termination bar at the edges.

6. Rubber roofs are soft and should not be subjected to routine foot traffic or any sharp objects.

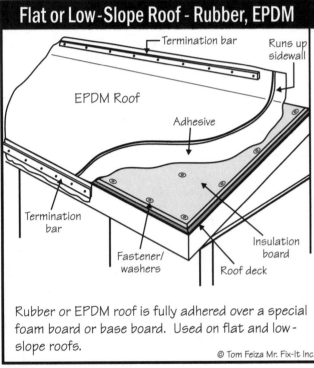

Flat or Low-Slope Roof - Rubber, EPDM

Termination bar
Runs up sidewall
EPDM Roof
Adhesive
Termination bar
Fastener/ washers
Roof deck
Insulation board

Rubber or EPDM roof is fully adhered over a special foam board or base board. Used on flat and low-slope roofs.

© Tom Feiza Mr. Fix-It Inc.

R019

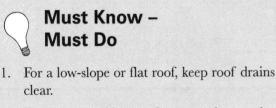

Must Know – Must Do

1. For a low-slope or flat roof, keep roof drains clear.

2. Don't use a rubber roof as a porch or patio.

3. Any patches or repairs should be done by a professional with compatible materials.

Roof Gutters and Drainage

1. With heavy soils and deep foundations, gutters and downspouts are used to collect roof water and direct it away from the foundation.

2. Gutters must be kept clean to prevent water damage.

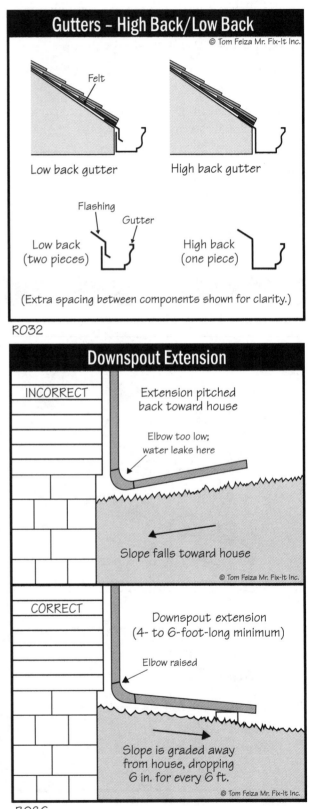

Gutters – High Back/Low Back

© Tom Feiza Mr. Fix-It Inc.

Felt
Low back gutter
High back gutter
Flashing
Gutter
Low back (two pieces)
High back (one piece)

(Extra spacing between components shown for clarity.)

R032

Downspout Extension

INCORRECT

Extension pitched back toward house

Elbow too low; water leaks here

Slope falls toward house

© Tom Feiza Mr. Fix-It Inc.

CORRECT

Downspout extension (4- to 6-foot-long minimum)

Elbow raised

Slope is graded away from house, dropping 6 in. for every 6 ft.

© Tom Feiza Mr. Fix-It Inc.

B086

Roof Plumbing Vents

1. The plumbing drainage system requires open vent pipes through the roof that introduce air into the drainpipes and allow sewer gas to escape.

2. The vent pipes are flashed or connected to the roof with lead or metal and neoprene flashing.

3. The flashing should be continuous, without holes or gaps. Flashing laps under the roof covering.

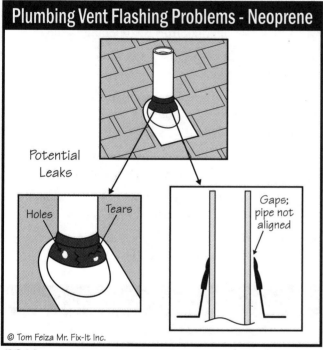

Plumbing Vent Flashing Problems - Neoprene

Potential Leaks

Holes   Tears

Gaps; pipe not aligned

© Tom Feiza Mr. Fix-It Inc.

R044

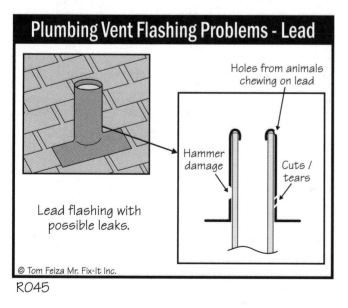

Plumbing Vent Flashing Problems - Lead

Holes from animals chewing on lead

Hammer damage   Cuts / tears

Lead flashing with possible leaks.

© Tom Feiza Mr. Fix-It Inc.

R045

Bituminous Membranes

1. In parts of the country prone to ice dams or any type of water backup on a roof, a bituminous membrane can solve leak problems.

2. Membranes are made by various manufacturers. The most common membrane is the Grace brand Ice and Water Shield.

3. The membrane seals around nail penetrations and prevents leaks.

4. The membrane is typically a thin sticky material that is laid on the roof from rolls.

5. Whenever there is a backup of water on an asphalt shingle roof (like an ice dam), there is the potential for a leak.

6. These membranes are used on overhangs and near gutters. They should extend up about two feet over the heated space.

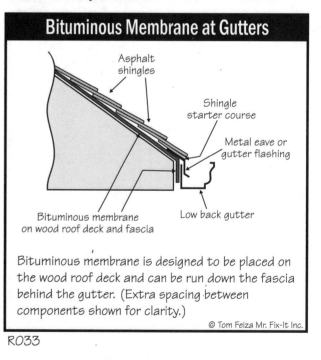

Bituminous Membrane at Gutters

Asphalt shingles

Shingle starter course

Metal eave or gutter flashing

Bituminous membrane on wood roof deck and fascia

Low back gutter

Bituminous membrane is designed to be placed on the wood roof deck and can be run down the fascia behind the gutter. (Extra spacing between components shown for clarity.)

© Tom Feiza Mr. Fix-It Inc.

R033

> ### Must Know – Must Do
>
> 1. Protect your home from ice dams with proper insulation and ventilation of the attic.
>
> 2. Protect your home from leaks by maintaining gutters and downspout systems.
>
> 3. During roof replacement, consider installing a membrane at areas with the potential for leaks.

Chapter 5 – Fireplace, Chimney

Masonry Chimney

1. A masonry (brick or stone) chimney safely moves the products of combustion to the outdoors.

2. Modern masonry chimneys are lined with a clay tile flue to control the products of combustion.

3. A chimney is used for wood- and gas-burning appliances, such as a fireplace, a furnace, and a gas water heater.

4. Some homes may have a larger chimney with multiple flues, like the chimney shown here with one flue for a fireplace and another for the heating plant.

5. Some modern gas-burning appliances are directly vented through a side wall without a chimney.

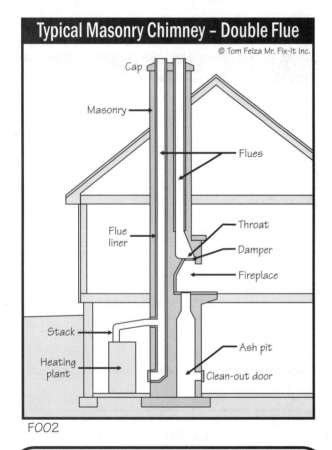

Typical Masonry Chimney – Double Flue
© Tom Feiza Mr. Fix-It Inc.

Cap
Masonry
Flues
Flue liner
Throat
Damper
Fireplace
Stack
Heating plant
Ash pit
Clean-out door

F002

Must Know – Must Do

1. A chimney should be cleaned and inspected on a routine basis.

2. The chimney must have a good crown and cap to protect it from water.

Masonry Fireplace Parts

1. A masonry (brick, stone) fireplace starts with a masonry foundation for support.

2. The fireplace is constructed with fire-resistant brick in the firebox.

3. The firebox controls combustion and allows combustion gas to flow up the chimney while reflecting heat into the room.

4. A metal damper controls the opening to the flue.

5. A hearth extension protects the wood frame from sparks and heat.

6. As an option, a fireplace may have an outside air supply to limit the amount of air and heat going up the chimney from the living space.

7. In general, a masonry fireplace creates big heat losses as heated air moves up the chimney.

8. A fireplace and chimney should be professionally cleaned on a routine basis.

9. Always close the damper when the fireplace is not in use to prevent heat loss up the chimney

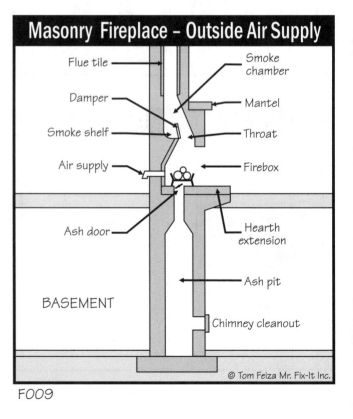

Masonry Fireplace – Outside Air Supply

Flue tile
Smoke chamber
Damper
Mantel
Smoke shelf
Throat
Air supply
Firebox
Ash door
Hearth extension
Ash pit
BASEMENT
Chimney cleanout
© Tom Feiza Mr. Fix-It Inc.

F009

Masonry Chimney Parts

1. The exposed top of a masonry chimney is subjected to weather extremes.

2. The top of a chimney must be watertight and able to shed water, or it will be damaged.

3. Water intrusion and freeze-thaw cycles are very damaging.

4. The chimney is protected from water and animals with a rain cap over the flue opening.

5. A solid concrete or stone cap that overhangs the chimney protects it from water.

6. A continuous clay tile liner protects the masonry from the products of combustion.

Rain Cap for Masonry Chimney

© Tom Feiza Mr. Fix-It Inc.

Rain cap or chimney cap

Flexible sealant

Solid concrete cap

3" thick

Drip edge

Brick

Clay flue liner

A rain cap or chimney cap protects the chimney from water and keeps animals out of the flue.

F030

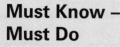

Must Know – Must Do

1. From the ground, using binoculars, inspect your chimney annually.

2. All mortar joints and brick should appear solid and tight.

3. If the chimney is used for a wood-burning appliance, it should be cleaned and checked on a routine basis.

Metal Chimneys

1. In newer construction, metal chimneys and metal flues are often used in place of masonry chimneys.

2. A metal chimney and metal flue are specially designed for the connected fireplace or gas appliance.

3. Often, a wood structure surrounds the metal flue.

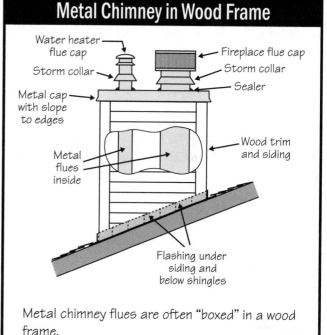

Metal Chimney in Wood Frame

Water heater flue cap

Storm collar

Metal cap with slope to edges

Metal flues inside

Fireplace flue cap

Storm collar

Sealer

Wood trim and siding

Flashing under siding and below shingles

Metal chimney flues are often "boxed" in a wood frame.

© Tom Feiza Mr. Fix-It Inc.

F031

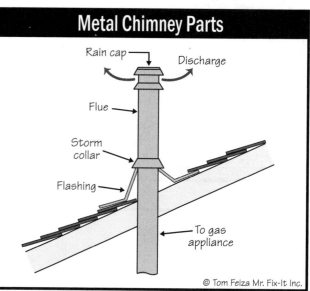

Metal Chimney Parts

Rain cap

Discharge

Flue

Storm collar

Flashing

To gas appliance

© Tom Feiza Mr. Fix-It Inc.

F029

Metal Prefabricated Fireplace

1. In modern construction, most fireplaces are prefabricated in a factory and then installed in a home.

2. These prefabricated fireplaces use a metal box and special flue.

3. The fireplace may be rated to burn wood or gas. Look for the label on the unit.

4. Many units use an outside air supply for combustion.

5. Some units have a circulating fan that moves room air around the metal firebox to transfer heat into the room.

6. Many units have faces of brick, stone or faux stone. These appear to be masonry fireplaces.

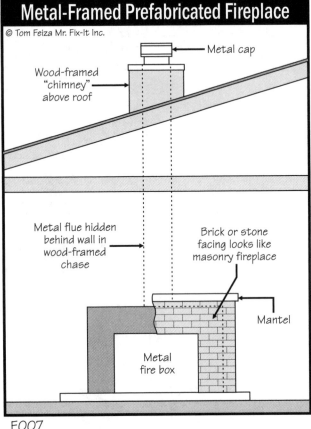

Metal-Framed Prefabricated Fireplace

© Tom Feiza Mr. Fix-It Inc.

Metal cap

Wood-framed "chimney" above roof

Metal flue hidden behind wall in wood-framed chase

Brick or stone facing looks like masonry fireplace

Mantel

Metal fire box

FOO7

Must Know – Must Do

1. Know how to operate the damper, as well as the outside air supply and gas valve if they are used on your fireplace.

2. Have the unit cleaned and checked on a routine basis.

Direct Vent Fireplace

1. Some modern gas fireplaces have a sealed combustion chamber and can be vented through a side wall.

2. Sealed combustion fireplaces are specially designed with a combustion air supply and a metal vent for the products of combustion.

3. Outside, on the wall adjacent to the fireplace, the metal vent will appear as a rectangular metal box with slots.

4. Many systems use one connection to the outside for an air supply and vent.

5. These units are very efficient heating appliances and often include a fan that circulates room air around the firebox to heat the living space.

6. Units are designed for a specific gas log set and controls.

7. A remote control or a room thermostat controls some units.

8. When the unit first starts, some condensation or fog may appear inside the glass cover.

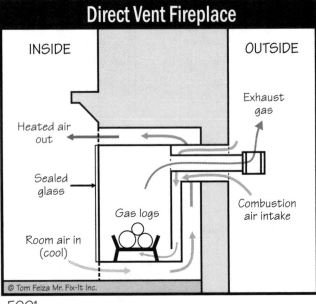

Direct Vent Fireplace

INSIDE   OUTSIDE

Heated air out

Exhaust gas

Sealed glass

Gas logs

Combustion air intake

Room air in (cool)

© Tom Feiza Mr. Fix-It Inc.

FOO1

Must Know – Must Do

1. Always follow the manufacturer's directions for operations and maintenance.

2. Be aware that the glass cover will be hot and can cause burns.

Warm Air Furnace

1. A warm air (forced air) furnace provides heat by burning gas or oil and circulating heated air within your home.

2. The fuel heats the inside of a heat exchanger, and the heat exchanger transfers heat to the air.

3. A blower or fan circulates air through the system into your home through supply and return ducts.

4. A thermostat automatically turns the system on and off based on the temperature set point in the heated space.

5. A 120-volt switch on or near the unit turns the furnace on and off.

6. The furnace has an air filter that requires routine maintenance.

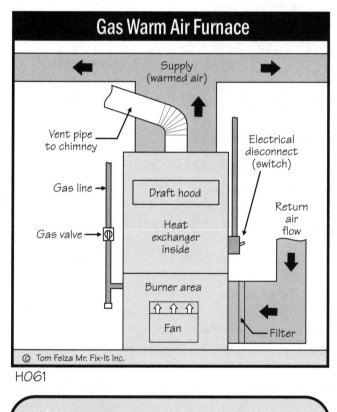

HO61

Must Know – Must Do

1. Locate the on-off switch and fuel valve.

2. Maintain the filter.

3. Arrange professional service yearly.

Forced Air Heating Systems

1. A forced air furnace may be located in the attic or garage when there is no basement or crawl space.

2. The duct distribution system is located in the attic, with supply grilles in the ceilings.

3. The filter may be in the unit's air return or in a large hallway return duct.

4. A horizontal flow furnace and ductwork may also be located in a crawl space.

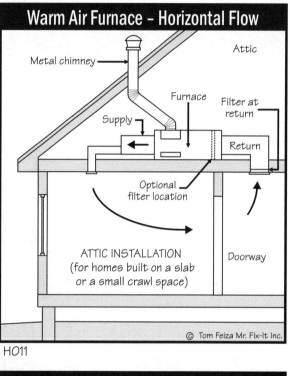

HO11

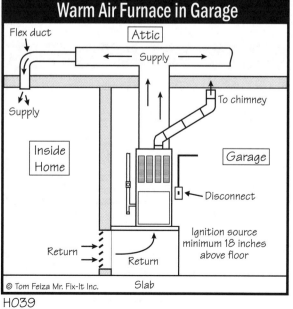

HO39

Forced Air Distribution Systems

1. With a forced air furnace, a supply and return duct system distributes heated air into the home.

2. A furnace in a basement has ducts in the basement; an attic or garage furnace has ducts in the attic; and a downflow furnace may have ducts in the floor slab.

3. Dampers in the systems can be adjusted to modify the air flow.

4. Some units allow adjustments for summer cooling and winter heating operation by adjusting the return duct openings.

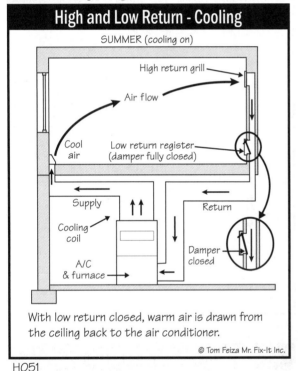

High and Low Return - Cooling

SUMMER (cooling on)

High return grill

Air flow

Cool air

Low return register (damper fully closed)

Supply

Return

Cooling coil

Damper closed

A/C & furnace

With low return closed, warm air is drawn from the ceiling back to the air conditioner.

© Tom Feiza Mr. Fix-It Inc.

H051

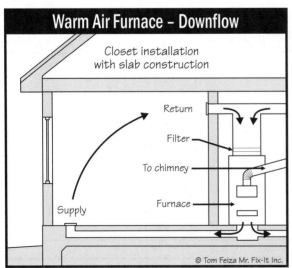

Warm Air Furnace – Downflow

Closet installation with slab construction

Return

Filter

To chimney

Furnace

Supply

© Tom Feiza Mr. Fix-It Inc.

H012

Heat Pump Systems

1. A heat pump transfers heat from the exterior air to a coil inside the forced air system.

2. A heat pump system may look like an air conditioning system.

3. A filter will be located in the forced air system.

4. A disconnect switch at the outside unit and at the main electrical panel will turn off the 240-volt power supply.

5. Below 40 degrees, the system may use electrical resistance heat or an alternative heat source.

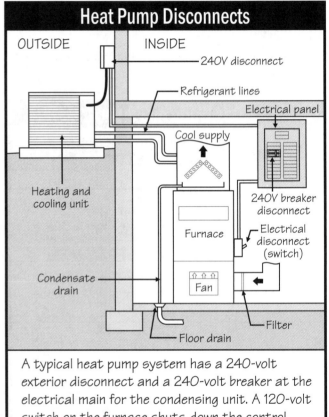

Heat Pump Disconnects

OUTSIDE   INSIDE

240V disconnect

Refrigerant lines

Electrical panel

Cool supply

Heating and cooling unit

240V breaker disconnect

Furnace

Electrical disconnect (switch)

Condensate drain

Fan

Filter

Floor drain

A typical heat pump system has a 240-volt exterior disconnect and a 240-volt breaker at the electrical main for the condensing unit. A 120-volt switch on the furnace shuts down the control system. A separate 120-volt breaker turns off the power to the furnace/fan/controls.

© Tom Feiza Mr. Fix-It Inc.

H057

Must Know – Must Do

1. Maintain the filter on the system.

2. Schedule yearly professional service.

Filtering for Forced Air Heating

1. Every forced air system has a filter to protect it from dirt.

2. Filters can be made of fiberglass, paper, carbon or a combination of materials.

3. Filters must be maintained to ensure proper air flow and energy efficiency.

4. Filters will be located somewhere in the duct return system, often next to the fan housing.

5. All filters must be installed with the correct orientation for air flow through the filter.

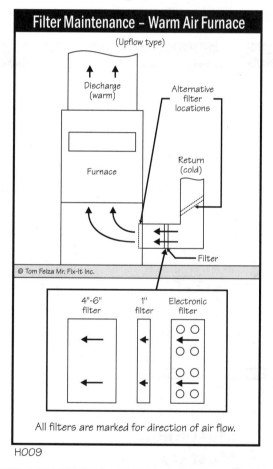

Filter Maintenance – Warm Air Furnace
(Upflow type)

Discharge (warm)

Alternative filter locations

Return (cold)

Furnace

Filter

© Tom Feiza Mr. Fix-It Inc.

| 4"-6" filter | 1" filter | Electronic filter |

All filters are marked for direction of air flow.

H009

Air Filter Types

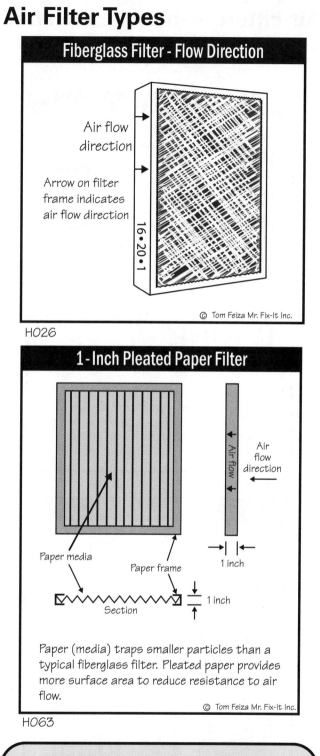

Fiberglass Filter - Flow Direction

Air flow direction

Arrow on filter frame indicates air flow direction

16•20•1

© Tom Feiza Mr. Fix-It Inc.

H026

1-Inch Pleated Paper Filter

Air flow direction

Paper media

Paper frame

1 inch

1 inch

Section

Paper (media) traps smaller particles than a typical fiberglass filter. Pleated paper provides more surface area to reduce resistance to air flow.

© Tom Feiza Mr. Fix-It Inc.

H063

💡 Must Know – Must Do

1. Maintain the filter properly, according to the type of filter and system.

2. Turn the unit off before changing the filter.

3. Always watch for the direction of air flow through the filter.

💡 Must Know – Must Do

1. Check and maintain 1-inch-thick filters monthly.

2. Watch for the correct air flow direction.

3. Be aware that pleated paper filters will remove more dust and dirt.

Air Filters – Higher Efficiency

1. The 4-inch or 6-inch filters usually are changed yearly.

2. The electronic filter is washed monthly.

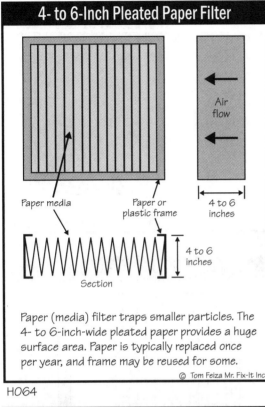

4- to 6-Inch Pleated Paper Filter

Paper media

Paper or plastic frame

Air flow

4 to 6 inches

4 to 6 inches

Section

Paper (media) filter traps smaller particles. The 4- to 6-inch-wide pleated paper provides a huge surface area. Paper is typically replaced once per year, and frame may be reused for some.

© Tom Feiza Mr. Fix-It Inc.

H064

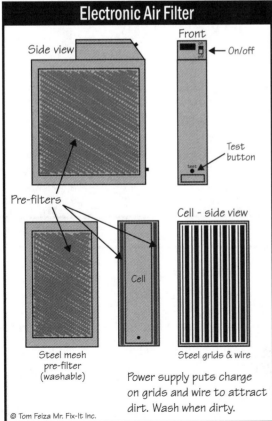

Electronic Air Filter

Side view

Front

On/off

Test button

Pre-filters

Cell - side view

Cell

Steel mesh pre-filter (washable)

Steel grids & wire

Power supply puts charge on grids and wire to attract dirt. Wash when dirty.

© Tom Feiza Mr. Fix-It Inc.

H029

Hydronic Heating System

1. A hydronic heating system or boiler heats water in a closed piping system.

2. The piping is connected to radiators or convectors to move heat into the conditioned space.

3. A thermostat in the conditioned space controls the system.

4. An expansion tank on the system holds excess water as the water warms and expands.

5. The heat source could be natural gas, propane, oil or electrical resistance.

6. A 120-volt switch on or near the unit can turn it off.

7. A pump circulates water through the system.

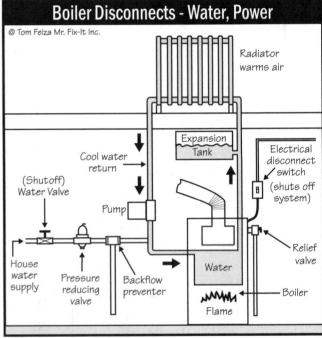

Boiler Disconnects - Water, Power

© Tom Feiza Mr. Fix-It Inc.

Radiator warms air

Cool water return

Expansion Tank

Electrical disconnect switch (shuts off system)

(Shutoff) Water Valve

Pump

House water supply

Pressure reducing valve

Backflow preventer

Water

Relief valve

Boiler

Flame

H038

💡 **Must Know – Must Do**

1. Be alert for leaks or strange noises.

2. Oil the circulation pump with a few drops of oil twice per year if there is an oil fitting.

3. Arrange for yearly professional service.

Steam Heating Systems

1. A steam boiler produces steam, and the steam is routed through a piping system to radiators (one-pipe system).

2. A 120-volt switch on or near the boiler can turn it off.

3. The boiler has a water supply valve.

4. The heat source could be natural gas, propane, oil or electrical resistance.

5. A thermostat in the conditioned space controls the system.

6. The system's air vents must be maintained.

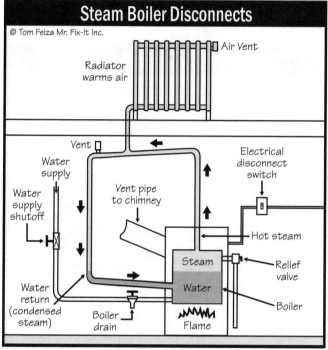

Steam Boiler Disconnects

© Tom Feiza Mr. Fix-It Inc.

Air Vent
Radiator warms air
Vent
Electrical disconnect switch
Water supply
Water supply shutoff
Vent pipe to chimney
Hot steam
Steam
Relief valve
Water
Water return (condensed steam)
Boiler drain
Flame
Boiler

H040

> ## Must Know – Must Do
>
> 1. Schedule professional service yearly.
>
> 2. Cold radiators often indicate a vent problem.
>
> 3. Water should be drained from the system monthly to remove contaminates; check with your professional service person for the correct routine.

Fuel Oil Heating Systems

1. Fuel oil is used as an energy source for heating homes and domestic hot water.

2. The burner pressurizes oil, sprays it through a small nozzle, and provides a spark and air supply for complete combustion.

3. Because of the resulting high temperatures, the flame is contained in a refractory.

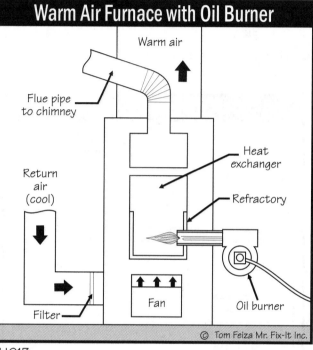

Warm Air Furnace with Oil Burner

Warm air
Flue pipe to chimney
Heat exchanger
Return air (cool)
Refractory
Filter
Fan
Oil burner

© Tom Feiza Mr. Fix-It Inc.

H013

> ## Must Know – Must Do
>
> 1. Schedule professional service and adjustment yearly.
>
> 2. Watch for soot in or around the system, which indicates a problem.
>
> 3. Keep in mind that there should never be a fuel oil leak or odor.
>
> 4. Never let the system run out of fuel oil; this will damage the system.

Ductwork – Dampers

1. Forced air duct systems have dampers that can be re-positioned to control air flow.

2. Typically, dampers are small plates tipped inside the ductwork in an open, closed or partially closed position.

3. The screwdriver slot or lever on the damper shaft indicates the damper's position.

4. Often, dampers are set once and then never changed, except possibly for a switch from heating to cooling.

5. Dampers can be used to redirect flow to cold or warm rooms.

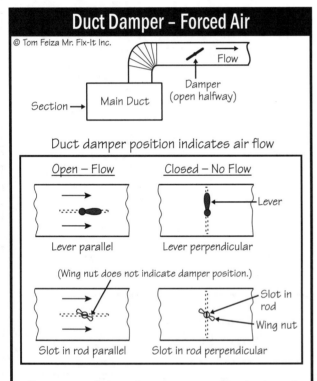

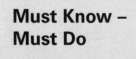

Duct Damper – Forced Air

© Tom Feiza Mr. Fix-It Inc.

Duct damper position indicates air flow

Two types of duct dampers: one with slot in rod and wing nut, and one with handle or lever.

H042

Must Know – Must Do

1. The homeowner can make slight adjustments to dampers.

2. Seasonal changes can be made as needed.

3. A professional should do major adjustments.

High and Low Returns – Cold Climates

1. Some systems have high and low return grills.

2. In some systems, adjusting the lower return grill damper also opens or closes the upper return grill duct.

3. During heating, the lower return should be open to draw cool air back to the furnace.

4. During cooling, the upper return should be open to return warm air to the cooling system.

5. In many cases, only a high return is provided.

6. For systems without a basement duct system, you will not find high and low returns.

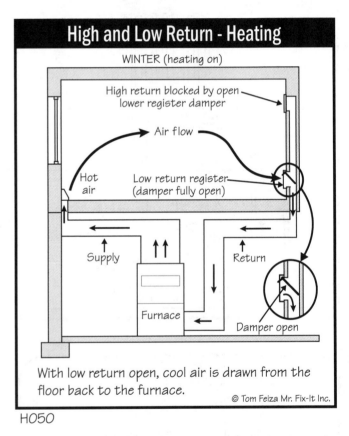

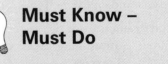

High and Low Return - Heating

With low return open, cool air is drawn from the floor back to the furnace.

© Tom Feiza Mr. Fix-It Inc.

H050

Must Know – Must Do

1. Check for high and low returns, and understand your system.

2. Make seasonal adjustments as needed.

Thermostat – Heating and Cooling

1. The thermostat is located in the conditioned space. It senses the room temperature.

2. A switch on the thermostat allows you to set the system for heating or cooling, or to turn off the system.

3. There is also a switch that turns on only the fan. To use this, set it to fan "on."

4. When the fan switch is set to "auto," the fan will cycle on and off as needed.

5. Some thermostats are for heating only, such as those for boilers.

6. Thermostats for heat pumps may have additional controls for backup heating.

7. Most thermostats provide a full-on or full-off control, not a variable heating or cooling rate.

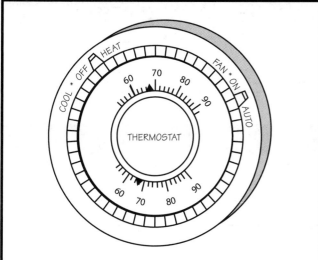

Heat - Cool Thermostat

H023

Must Know – Must Do

1. If there is no heat or cooling, check the thermostat to make sure it is set for heating or cooling, not at "off."

Digital Thermostat

1. The thermostat is located in the conditioned space. It uses digital sensors to sense the room temperature.

2. The thermostat turns the heating or cooling system on as the room temperature varies a few degrees from the set point.

3. A switch on the thermostat allows you to set the system for heating or cooling, or to turn off the system.

4. There is also a switch that turns on only the fan. To use this, set it to fan "on."

5. When the fan switch is set to "auto," the fan will cycle on and off as needed.

6. Digital thermostats often provide the option of programming daily temperature settings.

7. Most thermostats provide a full-on or full-off control, not a variable heating or cooling rate.

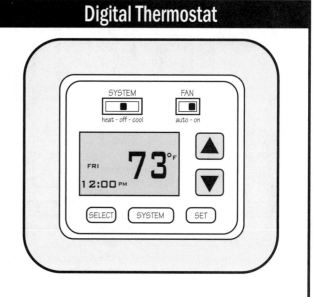

Digital Thermostat

Typical digital thermostat program for automatic temperature settings based on day of week and time. Many variations exist.

© Tom Feiza Mr. Fix-It Inc.

H025

Must Know – Must Do

1. If there is no heat or cooling, check the thermostat to make sure it is set for heating or cooling, not at "off."

Humidifier System and Controls

1. In cold climates and older homes, a central humidification system adds moisture to the air circulated by a forced air system during the winter.

2. The humidifier typically consists of a wet panel in the forced air stream that adds moisture as warm air moves through it.

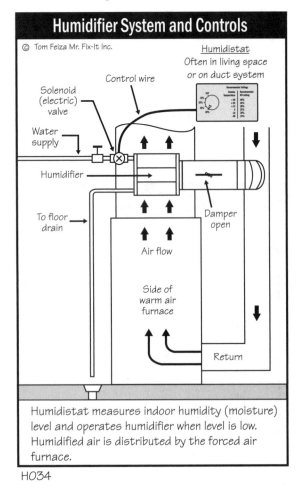

Humidistat measures indoor humidity (moisture) level and operates humidifier when level is low. Humidified air is distributed by the forced air furnace.

H034

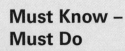

Must Know – Must Do

1. Watch for water leaks.
2. Keep the drain line clear.
3. Check whether your system has a bypass duct damper that needs to be adjusted seasonally.
4. If condensation forms on your windows in the winter, lower the humidity setting.
5. Routinely service the unit and change the water panel.

Heat System Disconnects

1. All heating and cooling equipment will have disconnects for the electrical, gas, oil, and water.

2. The electrical switch will shut down the system.

3. Understand the valves and switches, and tag them.

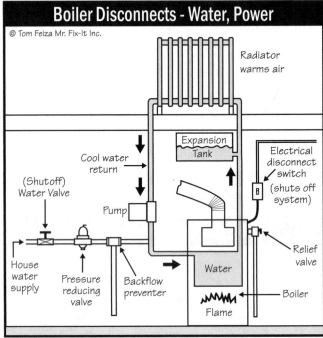

H038

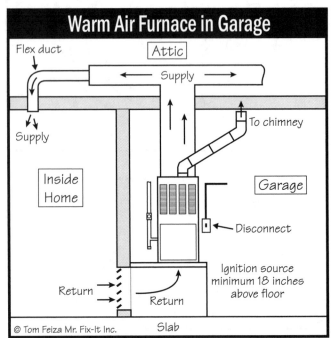

H039

Chapter 7 – Air Conditioning

Air Conditioning

1. A central air conditioning system uses an exterior coil and fan and an interior coil and fan to move indoor heat to the outdoors.

2. The interior coil cools air that is forced through it by the fan.

3. The exterior unit rejects heat into the outdoors.

4. The system is controlled by a thermostat in the cooled space that automatically cycles the system on and off to maintain the desired temperature.

5. Indoors, humidity in the air condenses on the cold coil. This water collects in a pan and must be drained from the system.

6. The filter near the indoor coil must be routinely cleaned or replaced.

Air Conditioning – Fan Unit Locations

1. An air conditioning system may have its cooling coil and fan system in the attic, garage or crawl space.

2. Some air conditioners are combined with a heating unit in a closet installation. This is typical for condo units.

3. See Air Conditioning information at left for operational information and Must Know – Must Do tips.

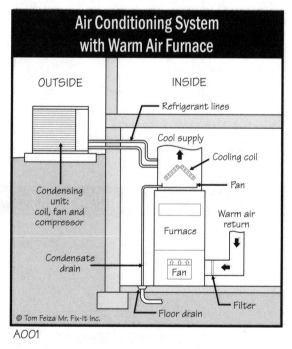

AO01

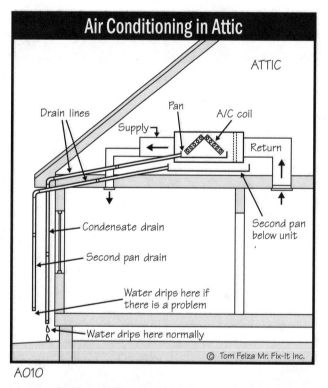

AO10

Must Know – Must Do

1. Clean the filter as needed.

2. Keep the drain line open, and watch for leaks.

3. Make sure the exterior coil is free of plants and debris.

4. Arrange for professional service yearly.

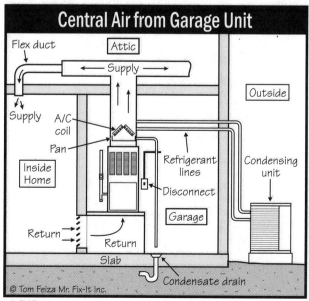

AO12

Cooling – Heat Pump

1. A heat pump looks and operates like a central air conditioning system, except that it can also cycle in reverse to provide heating.

2. The heat pump has a coil, fan, and filter inside.

3. As indoor air cools, water condenses from it. This water collects in a pan and drains away through a drain line.

4. For warm air heating, the heat pump transfers heat from an exterior coil to an interior coil.

5. The heat pump uses electricity to operate its refrigeration compressor.

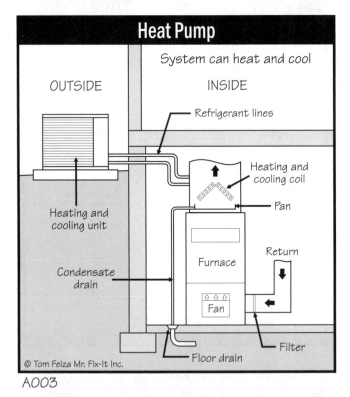

Heat Pump

System can heat and cool

OUTSIDE — INSIDE

Refrigerant lines

Heating and cooling coil

Pan

Heating and cooling unit

Furnace

Return

Condensate drain

Fan

Filter

Floor drain

© Tom Feiza Mr. Fix-It Inc.

A003

Must Know – Must Do

1. Keep the filter clean.

2. Keep the drain line open.

3. Watch for leaks.

4. Keep plants and debris away from the exterior coil.

5. Arrange for professional service yearly.

Air Conditioning Leaks

1. As an air conditioner coil cools air, water condenses on the coil, collects in a pan and drains away.

2. Watch for leaks, and always keep the drain line clear.

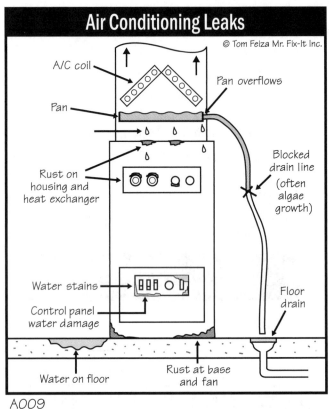

Air Conditioning Leaks

© Tom Feiza Mr. Fix-It Inc.

A/C coil

Pan overflows

Pan

Rust on housing and heat exchanger

Blocked drain line (often algae growth)

Water stains

Control panel water damage

Floor drain

Water on floor

Rust at base and fan

A009

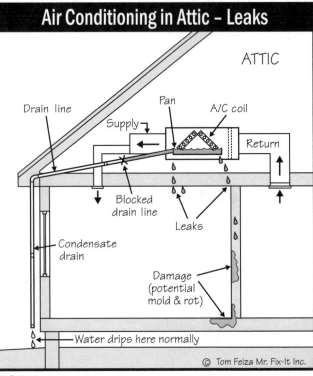

Air Conditioning in Attic – Leaks

ATTIC

Drain line

Pan

A/C coil

Supply

Return

Blocked drain line

Leaks

Condensate drain

Damage (potential mold & rot)

Water drips here normally

© Tom Feiza Mr. Fix-It Inc.

A011

Refrigeration Cycle

1. A typical air conditioning system uses refrigeration to cool air.

2. In the exterior unit, a compressor turns cool refrigerant gas (Freon) into hot, high-pressure gas.

3. This hot gas runs through a set of coils, dissipates heat, and condenses into a liquid.

4. The liquid flows through an expansion valve. As it does so, it evaporates, becoming cold, low-pressure gas.

5. The cold gas runs through another set of coils. These coils allow the gas to absorb heat, cooling the air that flows across them.

6. This cooled air is distributed to the interior of your home.

7. The cold gas flows back into the compressor and the cycle starts over.

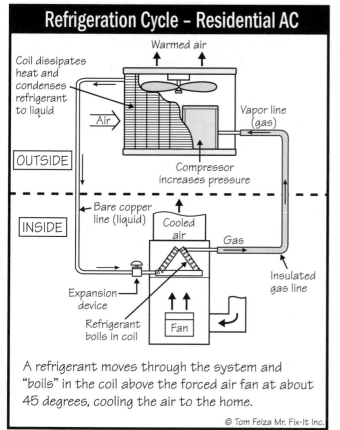

Refrigeration Cycle – Residential AC

Warmed air

Coil dissipates heat and condenses refrigerant to liquid

Air

OUTSIDE

Vapor line (gas)

Compressor increases pressure

INSIDE

Bare copper line (liquid)

Cooled air

Gas

Expansion device

Insulated gas line

Refrigerant boils in coil

Fan

A refrigerant moves through the system and "boils" in the coil above the forced air fan at about 45 degrees, cooling the air to the home.

© Tom Feiza Mr. Fix-It Inc.

A032

Air Conditioning Condenser Maintenance

1. Keep the exterior condenser clean and free of lint.

2. Make sure the exterior condenser is level.

3. Keep plants away from the exterior unit, since air must be allowed to flow freely through the exterior coil.

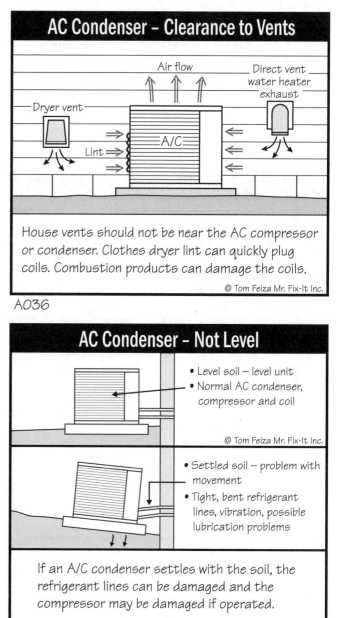

AC Condenser – Clearance to Vents

Air flow

Direct vent water heater exhaust

Dryer vent

A/C

Lint

House vents should not be near the AC compressor or condenser. Clothes dryer lint can quickly plug coils. Combustion products can damage the coils.

© Tom Feiza Mr. Fix-It Inc.

A036

AC Condenser – Not Level

• Level soil – level unit
• Normal AC condenser, compressor and coil

© Tom Feiza Mr. Fix-It Inc.

• Settled soil – problem with movement
• Tight, bent refrigerant lines, vibration, possible lubrication problems

If an A/C condenser settles with the soil, the refrigerant lines can be damaged and the compressor may be damaged if operated.

A037

Evaporative Cooler – Swamp Cooler

1. An evaporative cooler draws warm, dry outdoor air across a wet pad to cool the air.

2. The unit cools through evaporation of water – just as a human body cools when water evaporates from the skin.

3. The cooled air is blown into the home.

4. The system may be mounted on the roof or on a sidewall. Ductwork is often used to distribute the cooled air into the home.

5. Windows or vents must be open to allow air to move through the home.

6. A water supply and automatic float add water to the system pan, and an internal pump soaks the pad.

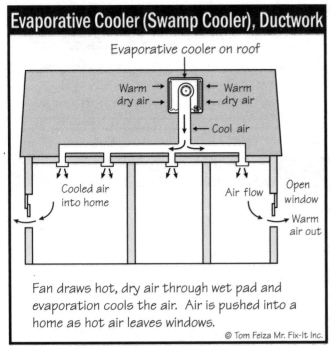

Evaporative Cooler (Swamp Cooler), Ductwork

Evaporative cooler on roof

Warm dry air → ← Warm dry air

← Cool air

Cooled air into home

Air flow

Open window

Warm air out

Fan draws hot, dry air through wet pad and evaporation cools the air. Air is pushed into a home as hot air leaves windows.

© Tom Feiza Mr. Fix-It Inc.

A027

Must Know – Must Do

1. The system needs periodic cleaning, since it can collect dirt from the outside air.

2. Watch for leaks, and monitor the water level in the unit.

3. Have the unit professionally serviced routinely.

Evaporative Cooler Details

1. An evaporative cooler draws warm, dry outdoor air across a wet pad to cool the air.

2. The unit cools through evaporation of water – just as a human body cools when water evaporates from the skin.

3. A water supply and automatic float add water to a pan below the evaporative pad.

4. An internal pump in the pan soaks the pad with water.

5. A fan moves exterior air across the wet pad and into the home.

6. The system can collect dirt from outdoor air and may even distribute dirt into the home, so it must be cleaned routinely.

7. An evaporative cooler will only work in hot, dry climates – not with humid exterior conditions.

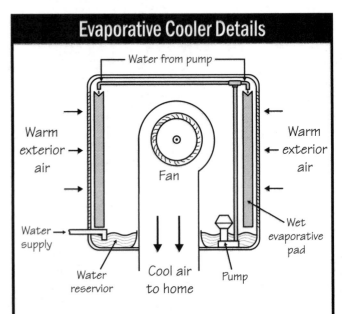

Evaporative Cooler Details

Water from pump

Warm exterior air

Warm exterior air

Fan

Water supply

Water reservoir

Cool air to home

Pump

Wet evaporative pad

Warm, dry air is drawn across a wet pad by fan. Water evaporates from the pad and cools the air. The pump wets the pads and a water supply fills the reservoir pan with a float for control.

© Tom Feiza Mr. Fix-It Inc.

A026

Natural Gas

1. Natural gas typically is fed to a home through underground distribution piping.

2. A gas meter is located either outdoors or indoors.

3. A valve at the meter turns off all gas to the home.

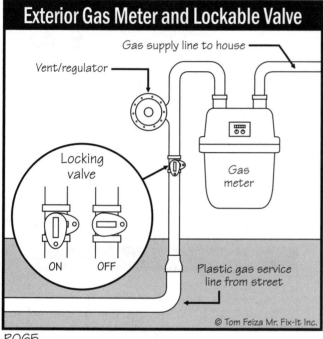

Exterior Gas Meter and Lockable Valve

Gas supply line to house

Vent/regulator

Locking valve

ON   OFF

Gas meter

Plastic gas service line from street

© Tom Feiza Mr. Fix-It Inc.

P065

Must Know – Must Do

1. Know the distinctive odor of natural gas. The odor identifies leaks.

2. If you smell gas anywhere in your home:

   a. Get everyone out of the house.

   b. Don't light matches or use electrical switches or devices.

   c. Call the gas company from a neighbor's house.

   d. Once outside, turn off the gas main. It is located near the meter. Give the valve a quarter-turn with a wrench until the valve is perpendicular to the piping.

   e. Wait for help from the gas company.

Natural Gas Distribution, Valves

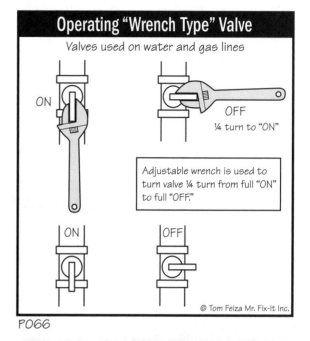

Operating "Wrench Type" Valve

Valves used on water and gas lines

ON

OFF
¼ turn to "ON"

Adjustable wrench is used to turn valve ¼ turn from full "ON" to full "OFF."

ON   OFF

© Tom Feiza Mr. Fix-It Inc.

P066

Typical Water Heater Parts – Gas

To chimney

Hot water out

Shutoff valve

Black iron gas supply pipe

Cold water in

Temperature and pressure relief valve

Gas shutoff

Water in tank

Temperature/ gas control valve

Dip tube

Burner

Drip leg

Drain valve

© Tom Feiza Mr. Fix-It Inc.

P082

Must Know – Must Do

1. All gas appliances must have a readily accessible shutoff valve nearby.

2. Locate and tag this valve for each gas appliance.

3. Know how to turn off the gas valve.

Fuel Oil

1. Fuel oil is often used as an energy source for space heating and domestic hot water.

2. Fuel oil tanks can be located in the basement, underground, or outside.

3. Fuel oil tanks have a fill and vent line.

4. The vent allows air to move out of the tank as it is filled.

5. Fuel from the tank flows through a shutoff valve and filter.

6. The fuel line from the tank to the appliance will often be made of flexible copper.

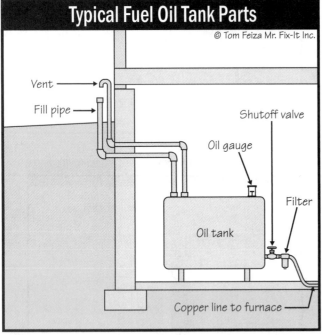

Typical Fuel Oil Tank Parts

© Tom Feiza Mr. Fix-It Inc.

Vent
Fill pipe
Shutoff valve
Oil gauge
Filter
Oil tank
Copper line to furnace

P123

Must Know – Must Do

1. Locate and know how to operate the shutoff valve.

2. Watch for leaks; the oil tank, piping and valve should never leak.

3. Never run the tank dry. This will damage the oil burners.

Propane

1. Propane gas is stored on site as liquid in a pressurized tank.

2. The propane tank is typically owned, maintained and filled by a service company.

3. Propane flows from the tank as gas through a valve and piping system.

4. If you smell propane gas anywhere in your home:

   a. Get everyone out of the house.

   b. Don't light matches or use electrical switches or devices.

   c. Call the propane service company from a neighbor's house.

   d. Once outside, turn off the gas main. It is located on the tank or at the spot where the pipe enters your home. Give the valve a quarter-turn with a wrench until the valve is perpendicular to the piping.

   e. Wait for help from the propane service company.

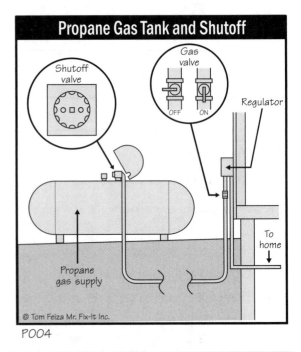

Propane Gas Tank and Shutoff

Gas valve
Shutoff valve
OFF   ON
Regulator
To home
Propane gas supply

© Tom Feiza Mr. Fix-It Inc.

P004

Must Know – Must Do

1. Locate and know how to operate the shutoff valve at the main tank.

2. Each gas appliance will have a shutoff valve located nearby. Know how to operate the valve.

Electrical

1. See the "Electricity" chapter for more details on the electrical service to your home.

2. Electrical energy is brought into a home through overhead or underground feed wires at 240 volts.

3. The electrical system is grounded through earth grounds and plumbing pipes for safety.

4. The main electrical panel provides wire overload protection with circuit breakers or fuses to prevent overheating the wires.

5. If a circuit breaker trips, don't reset it unless you have identified the specific problem.

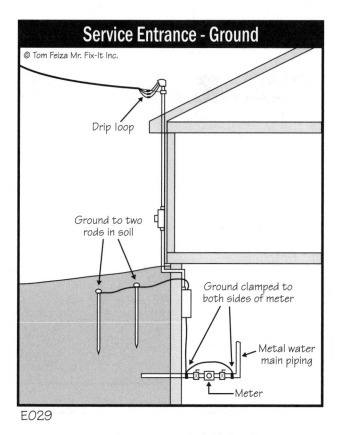

Service Entrance - Ground

© Tom Feiza Mr. Fix-It Inc.

Drip loop

Ground to two rods in soil

Ground clamped to both sides of meter

Metal water main piping

Meter

E029

Must Know – Must Do

1. At the main panel, identify the breaker or fuses and what they control.

2. Never disturb the overhead wires or the electrical meter.

3. Only qualified electricians should work on the system.

Gas Shutoff

1. All heating equipment and gas appliances will have a gas valve located on the gas line near the appliance. Tag this valve.

2. Some of these valves operate with a wrench, and some have a handle.

3. If the valve is old, corroded or damaged, have a professional replace it.

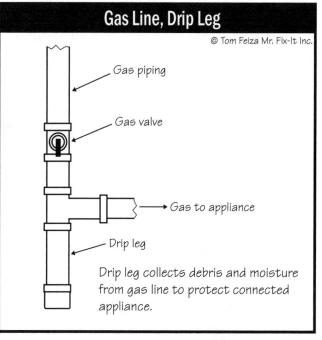

Gas Line, Drip Leg

© Tom Feiza Mr. Fix-It Inc.

Gas piping

Gas valve

Gas to appliance

Drip leg

Drip leg collects debris and moisture from gas line to protect connected appliance.

P043

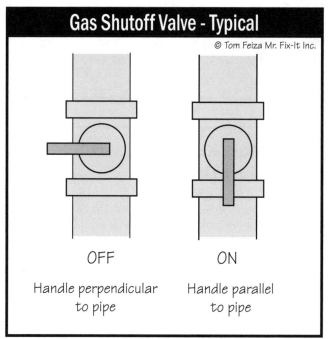

Gas Shutoff Valve - Typical

© Tom Feiza Mr. Fix-It Inc.

OFF
Handle perpendicular to pipe

ON
Handle parallel to pipe

P076

Chapter 9 – Plumbing

Water Supply – Municipal, Cold Climate

1. In a cold climate, the municipal (city) water supply line runs beneath the street and feeds underground into the basement.

2. The water supply must be below the frost line, so it lies several feet below grade.

3. The city's shutoff (curb) valve is located between the street and the home. It can be reached with a special long-handled wrench.

4. There will be a meter in the basement with a water shutoff near the meter.

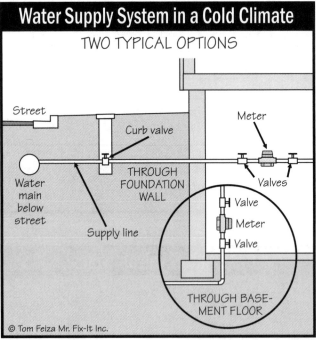

Water Supply System in a Cold Climate
TWO TYPICAL OPTIONS

Street · Curb valve · Meter · THROUGH FOUNDATION WALL · Valves · Water main below street · Supply line · Valve · Meter · Valve · THROUGH BASEMENT FLOOR

© Tom Feiza Mr. Fix-It Inc.

P005

Must Know – Must Do

1. Identify and tag the main water shutoff, and be sure everyone in the home knows how to turn off the water.

2. If the main valve is old or rusted, have it serviced by a plumber to make sure it will work when needed.

3. Watch for leaks or drips in the system.

Water Supply – Municipal, Warm Climate

1. In a warm climate, the city water supply runs beneath the street, just below the soil surface.

2. The main water valve may be located outside where the main enters the home.

3. The meter and a shutoff valve are often located in a small meter box just below the soil surface, near the street.

4. Beyond the meter, water is distributed throughout the home with steel, copper or plastic piping.

5. Valves inside the home isolate exterior hose connections and various appliances and fixtures.

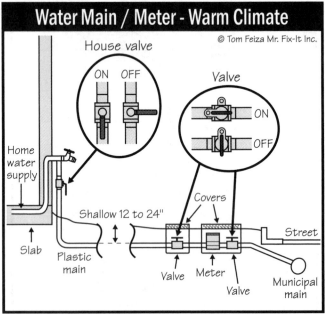

Water Main / Meter - Warm Climate

© Tom Feiza Mr. Fix-It Inc.

House valve · ON · OFF · Valve · ON · OFF · Home water supply · Covers · Slab · Shallow 12 to 24" · Street · Plastic main · Valve · Meter · Valve · Municipal main

P063

Must Know – Must Do

1. Identify and tag the main water shutoff, and be sure everyone in the home knows how to turn off the water.

2. If the main valve is old or rusted, have it serviced by a plumber to make sure it will work when needed.

3. Watch for leaks or drips in the system.

Water Supply – Private Well

1. With a private well, water is supplied by a well casing driven into the water table in the ground.

2. Most systems use a submersible pump in the well casing below the water, but shallow systems may use a pump mounted on the surface just above the well casing.

3. The system includes a pressure tank that holds air and water, providing a steady water supply.

4. Air in the tank pushes water into the home, reducing the need to operate the pump.

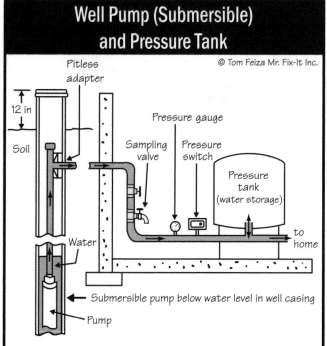

Well Pump (Submersible) and Pressure Tank

© Tom Feiza Mr. Fix-It Inc.

Pitless adapter

12 in

Soil

Pressure gauge

Sampling valve

Pressure switch

Pressure tank (water storage)

to home

Water

Submersible pump below water level in well casing

Pump

Pressure switch turns pump on and off to maintain pressure of 40 to 60 PSI with water stored in pressure tank. Water flows in and out of tank against air cushion.

P055

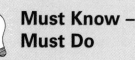

Must Know – Must Do

1. Tag the main valve and the pump switch. Make sure all the adults in your home know how to turn off the water and power.

2. Have the water tested routinely.

Water Distribution with Basement – Cold Climate

1. Water enters the home underground to a main water shutoff and water meter.

2. The water main will be a minimum of 3/4 inch diameter in newer homes and may be made of steel, copper or plastic.

3. Many meters have a remote usage indicator or radio frequency transmitter for ease of reading the meter without access to the basement.

4. The water distribution piping may be copper, steel, plastic or a combination of materials.

5. Locate shutoff valves for exterior hose connections, the water heater, and all major plumbing runs.

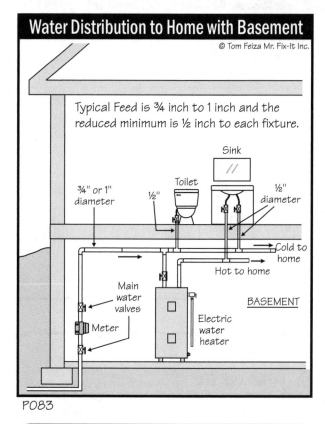

Water Distribution to Home with Basement

© Tom Feiza Mr. Fix-It Inc.

Typical Feed is ¾ inch to 1 inch and the reduced minimum is ½ inch to each fixture.

Sink

Toilet

¾" or 1" diameter

½"

½" diameter

Cold to home

Hot to home

Main water valves

Meter

Electric water heater

BASEMENT

P083

Must Know – Must Do

1. Locate the main water valve and know how to turn the water off. Be sure all adults in the home know how to do this.

2. Operate the main valve a few times per year – but if it is old and corroded, have a plumber repair it first.

Water Distribution with Slab – Warm Climate

1. Often, water enters the home through a pipe buried just below the surface of the soil.

2. The main water shutoff may be outside where the water main enters your home.

3. The main water shutoff and meter may be located in a shallow box near the street.

4. The water main will be a minimum of 3/4 inch for a newer home and may be made of copper or plastic.

5. Shutoff valves for hose connections, fixtures and major plumbing runs will be located inside the home.

Water Distribution with Crawl Space

1. Water enters the home underground to a main water shutoff and water meter in the crawl space.

2. The water main will be a minimum of 3/4 inch in newer homes and may be made of copper or plastic.

3. Many meters have a remote usage indicator or radio frequency transmitter for ease of reading the meter without access to the basement.

4. Locate shutoff valves for exterior hose connections, the water heater, and all major plumbing runs.

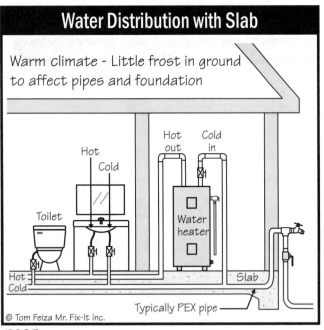

Water Distribution with Slab

Warm climate - Little frost in ground to affect pipes and foundation

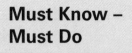

© Tom Feiza Mr. Fix-It Inc.

P085

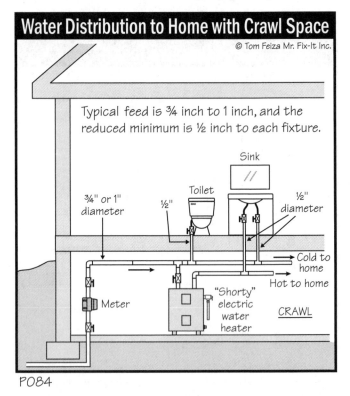

Water Distribution to Home with Crawl Space

© Tom Feiza Mr. Fix-It Inc.

Typical feed is ¾ inch to 1 inch, and the reduced minimum is ½ inch to each fixture.

P084

💡 Must Know – Must Do

1. Locate the main water valve and know how to turn the water off. Be sure all adults in the home know how to do this.

2. Operate the main valve a few times per year – but if it is old and corroded, have a plumber repair it first.

💡 Must Know – Must Do

1. Locate the main water valve and know how to turn the water off. Be sure all adults in the home know how to do this.

2. Operate the main valve a few times per year – but if it is old and corroded, have a plumber repair it first.

Drainage, Waste and Vent System

1. Once water is used, it drains away through a drainage, waste and vent system (DWV).

2. Older systems will be made of lead, steel, copper or cast iron. Newer systems will be made of plastic.

3. Pipes vary in size from 1 to 4 inches and are pitched to aid in the flow of water out of the system.

4. An open pipe (vent) at the top lets air enter the system, helping water drain freely from the piping.

5. A "trap" which traps water and prevents sewer gas from entering your home protects each fixture.

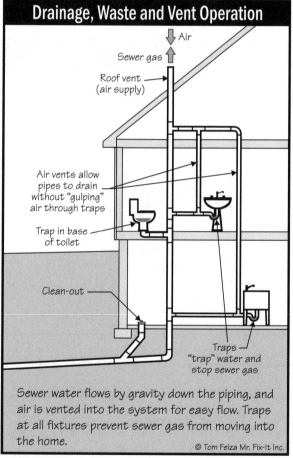

Drainage, Waste and Vent Operation

Sewer water flows by gravity down the piping, and air is vented into the system for easy flow. Traps at all fixtures prevent sewer gas from moving into the home.

© Tom Feiza Mr. Fix-It Inc.

P153

Must Know – Must Do

1. Never allow leaks in the system.

2. If water ever backs up, be aware that this water is contaminated, so thorough cleaning and disinfection is important.

Septic System

1. A septic system is a private wastewater treatment system.

2. Bacteria in the septic tank process wastewater that enters the system.

3. In the septic tank, grease and soap float to the top, and solids settle to the bottom.

4. The tank must be pumped on a routine basis to remove the scum and sludge.

5. As new wastewater enters the tank, partially treated water exits to an absorption field of perforated pipes in the soil.

6. Partially treated water is absorbed in the soil and evaporates into the air.

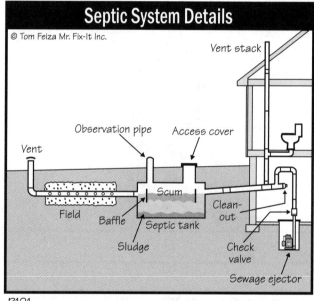

Septic System Details

© Tom Feiza Mr. Fix-It Inc.

P121

Must Know – Must Do

1. Have the septic tank pumped and inspected on a routine basis, normally once every year or two.

2. Don't put solids, like coffee grounds or bones, or oil, gasoline, or harsh chemicals into the system.

3. If the field is saturated and water appears on the surface of the soil, have the system checked by a professional.

Water Heater – Gas

1. Most water heaters consist of a storage tank with an energy source – gas, electric or oil.

2. The storage tank provides a reservoir of 30 to 75 gallons of hot water.

3. The water heater will begin reheating water as soon as the temperature in the tank drops below a set point.

4. The temperature and pressure valve on the side of the unit is a safety device to prevent high pressure and dangerous temperatures.

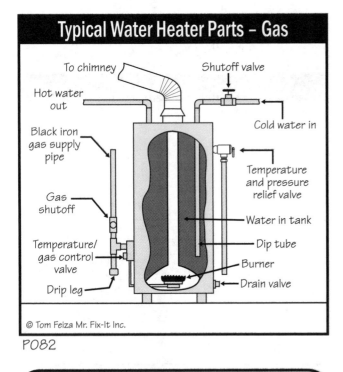

Typical Water Heater Parts – Gas

To chimney
Hot water out
Black iron gas supply pipe
Gas shutoff
Temperature/ gas control valve
Drip leg
Shutoff valve
Cold water in
Temperature and pressure relief valve
Water in tank
Dip tube
Burner
Drain valve

© Tom Feiza Mr. Fix-It Inc.

P082

Must Know – Must Do

1. Watch for leaks. Most water heater failures are due to a leaking tank.

2. Set the temperature as low as is comfortable.

3. Tag and test the shutoff valves for gas and water.

4. Never store gasoline near a water heater.

5. Drain sediment from the tank on a routine basis. Check the instructions for your unit.

Water Heater – Electric

1. Most water heaters consist of a storage tank with an energy source – gas, electric or oil.

2. The storage tank provides a reservoir of 40 to 75 gallons of hot water.

3. The water heater will begin reheating water with electrical resistance heaters as soon as the temperature in the tank drops below a set point.

4. Identify the cold-water inlet and shutoff valve.

5. Locate the electrical shutoff breaker in the main electrical panel in case of emergency.

6. The temperature and pressure valve on the side of the unit is a safety device to prevent high pressure and dangerous temperatures.

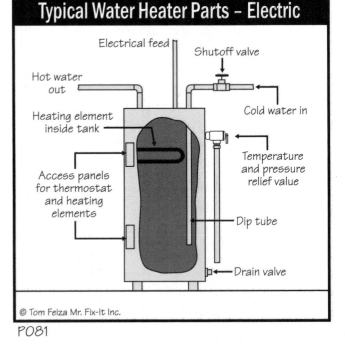

Typical Water Heater Parts – Electric

Electrical feed
Hot water out
Heating element inside tank
Access panels for thermostat and heating elements
Shutoff valve
Cold water in
Temperature and pressure relief value
Dip tube
Drain valve

© Tom Feiza Mr. Fix-It Inc.

P081

Must Know – Must Do

1. Watch for leaks. Most water heater failures are due to a leaking tank.

2. Tag and test the shutoff valves for water and electricity.

3. Drain sediment from the tank on a routine basis. Check the instructions for your unit.

Water Softener

1. If your home has hard water, a water softener is essential to remove calcium and magnesium so the water does not damage fixtures and leave spots on dishes.

2. The typical softener is connected to all hot water, and to all cold water except the kitchen sink cold and the hose faucets.

3. The system must be set to operate based on the hardness of the water and the number of people living in the home (gallon per person per day).

4. Older systems cycle with a time clock. Modern efficient systems meter water usage and cycle only as needed.

5. Valves on the piping or unit allow you to bypass the unit if necessary.

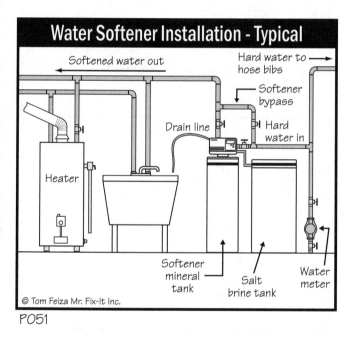

Water Softener Installation - Typical

Softened water out

Hard water to hose bibs

Softener bypass

Drain line

Hard water in

Heater

Softener mineral tank

Salt brine tank

Water meter

© Tom Feiza Mr. Fix-It Inc.

P051

Must Know – Must Do

1. Use the proper type of salt. Keep salt in the brine tank at all times.

2. If spots appear on dishes or water does not feel "slippery," this indicates that the softener is not working.

Water Backflow Prevention

Hose Bib – Backflow Prevention

© Tom Feiza Mr. Fix-It Inc.

Hose bib / sill cock (outside faucet)

Vacuum breaker (threads on)

Garden hose

Contaminated water

Dog's water dish

Add vacuum breaker to exterior hose bib to prevent backflow of contaminated water into drinking water. Required in many areas.

P034

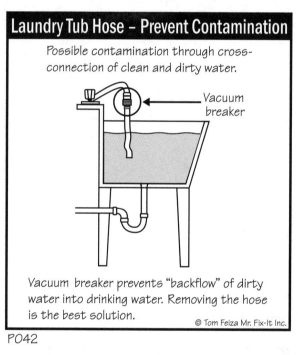

Laundry Tub Hose - Prevent Contamination

Possible contamination through cross-connection of clean and dirty water.

Vacuum breaker

Vacuum breaker prevents "backflow" of dirty water into drinking water. Removing the hose is the best solution.

© Tom Feiza Mr. Fix-It Inc.

P042

Must Know – Must Do

1. Backflow prevention devices must be used wherever there is a possible connection between contaminated water and drinking water.

2. Problems can occur with hoses, hot water boilers, sprinklers and other sources of contamination.

Typical Toilet

1. A typical toilet has a porcelain bowl that is filled with water. Beneath the bowl, water in the drain creates a "trap" to prevent sewer gas from entering the home.

2. The toilet tank is filled with water. A flush valve releases water into the bowl and trap.

3. After a flush, a float in the toilet tank drops, triggering water from the fill valve to fill the tank.

4. The fill valve also has a small tube leading to the overflow tube. This refills the trap as the tank fills.

5. The fill valve automatically shuts off as water raises the float to its original position.

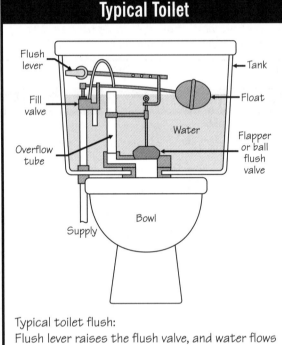

Typical Toilet

Typical toilet flush:
Flush lever raises the flush valve, and water flows from tank to bowl, flushing the toilet. Float drops with tank water level, and fill valve refills tank.

© Tom Feiza Mr. Fix-It Inc.

P025

Must Know – Must Do

1. Never allow a toilet to leak or drip.

2. Watch for stains around the base of the toilet. These could indicate a leak beneath the toilet.

3. The toilet should always be firmly mounted to the floor, or it may leak.

Shutoff Valves – Appliances

1. All appliances that use water have a shutoff valve.

2. The typical location of the valve for the dishwasher is shown here.

3. There will also be a shutoff valve for the refrigerator icemaker, washing machine, central humidifier, and other appliances that use water.

4. Test all valves to be sure they operate – but if a valve is corroded or difficult to operate, first have it checked or replaced by a plumber.

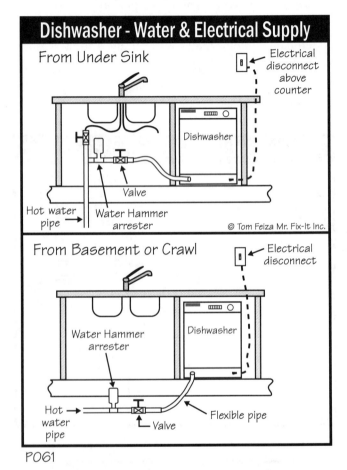

Dishwasher - Water & Electrical Supply

P061

Must Know – Must Do

1. Locate all valves for water supply to appliances.

2. Tag and test all valves.

3. Make sure everyone in the home knows how to turn off the water to appliances.

4. Make sure you know how to locate and operate the main water supply valve.

Garbage Disposal

1. A garbage disposal grinds food waste and washes it down the sewer system.

2. Always run water and turn on the disposal before placing waste in the unit.

3. Keep the water running for a few seconds after the unit is cleared.

4. A loud noise from the unit normally comes from something that should not be in the unit, such as a rag or a spoon.

5. If the unit "hums" and will not spin, something is stuck. Turn off the unit, clear the obstruction, and use the disposal wrench to turn the interior blades.

6. If the unit will not run, try pressing the reset button on the bottom of the unit.

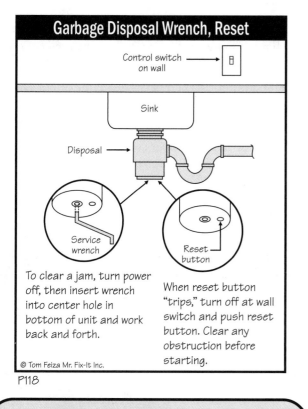

Garbage Disposal Wrench, Reset

Control switch on wall

Sink

Disposal

Service wrench

Reset button

To clear a jam, turn power off, then insert wrench into center hole in bottom of unit and work back and forth.

When reset button "trips," turn off at wall switch and push reset button. Clear any obstruction before starting.

© Tom Feiza Mr. Fix-It Inc.

P118

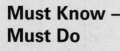
Must Know – Must Do

1. Always run a strong flow of cold water and start the disposal before you feed any waste into it.

2. Never put your hand in the disposal.

3. Know how to use the reset button and the service wrench.

Hose Faucets

1. A "hose bib" is an exterior faucet typically used for a hose connection.

2. There are two basic types: the frost-proof type with a long stem and the valve assembly inside the home's heated space, and the standard valve/bib.

3. During freezing conditions, the inside valve should be turned off and the outside valve opened. If there is a drain cap on the internal valve, open it.

4. During freezing conditions, hoses must be removed from hose bibs to prevent freezing.

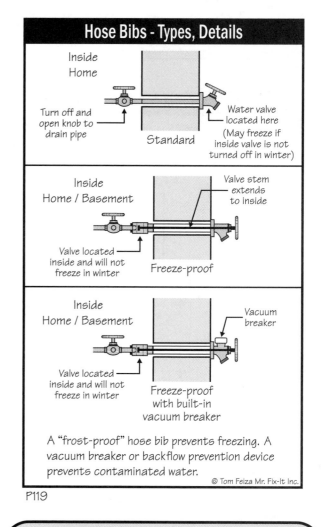

Hose Bibs - Types, Details

Inside Home

Turn off and open knob to drain pipe

Water valve located here (May freeze if inside valve is not turned off in winter)

Standard

Inside Home / Basement

Valve stem extends to inside

Valve located inside and will not freeze in winter

Freeze-proof

Inside Home / Basement

Vacuum breaker

Valve located inside and will not freeze in winter

Freeze-proof with built-in vacuum breaker

A "frost-proof" hose bib prevents freezing. A vacuum breaker or backflow prevention device prevents contaminated water.

© Tom Feiza Mr. Fix-It Inc.

P119

Must Know – Must Do

1. During freezing conditions, turn off water to the hose bib, and remove hoses.

2. Always be sure there is a backflow prevention device in place.

Pounding Pipes

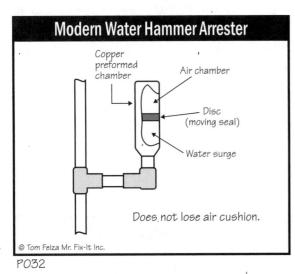

Modern Water Hammer Arrester

Copper preformed chamber

Air chamber

Disc (moving seal)

Water surge

Does not lose air cushion.

© Tom Feiza Mr. Fix-It Inc.

P032

Water Hammer Arresters

Old style – air chamber made with standard parts

Copper preformed chamber

¾" copper pipe about 12" high

¾" steel pipe about 12" high

© Tom Feiza Mr. Fix-It Inc.

P015

Must Know – Must Do

1. A water hammer arrester absorbs energy when water flow is quickly stopped.

2. The energy is absorbed by an air cushion in the arrester.

3. If your pipes pound when water turns off, this indicates a failed water hammer arrester or a missing arrester.

4. Older types provide only an air chamber; you can drain the system to restore the air cushion.

Sanitary and Storm Sewers

1. Modern municipal systems have separate storm and sanitary sewer systems.

2. The storm sewer is connected to grates in the street and to roof drainage. It carries rainwater to rivers and streams.

3. The sanitary sewer directs water from the home's wastewater drainage (from sinks, drains, and toilets) to a wastewater treatment plant.

4. Older cities may have combined sewers in which the sanitary and storm sewers are combined. This often causes excess flow into the system during heavy rains.

5. If there is a ditch in front of your home, it is likely used to drain storm water; you don't have a separate storm sewer system.

6. Sump pumps collect rainwater and should be discharged to the surface or to the storm sewer. Your municipality may have regulations on this.

7. Sump pumps should never discharge into a sanitary sewer or laundry tub.

8. Never dump paint, solvents or chemicals down the storm or sanitary sewer systems. Contact your local municipality for disposal options.

9. Your local municipality can provide assistance for understanding the specific design of your sewer systems.

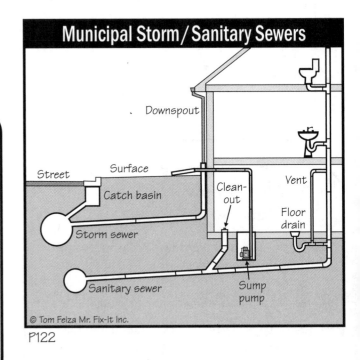

Municipal Storm / Sanitary Sewers

Downspout

Street

Surface

Catch basin

Storm sewer

Sanitary sewer

Clean-out

Vent

Floor drain

Sump pump

© Tom Feiza Mr. Fix-It Inc.

P122

Sanitary Pumps

1. Some homes appear to have two sump pumps in the basement floor.

2. Often one of these pumps is a sewage ejector.

3. A sewage ejector is used when the main sanitary sewer line exits the home through the basement wall and sanitary waste from the basement must be pumped up into the sanitary sewer.

4. Typically, a sewage ejector pump is in a sealed crock with a plumbing vent line.

5. Older sewage ejectors handling only a floor drain or laundry tub may not have a sealed cover.

6. The sanitary sewage ejector pump will be sized and designed to handle the type of waste entering the crock. Some are grinder pumps for solid waste.

7. Most basements with a private waste disposal system (septic system) will have a sewage ejector.

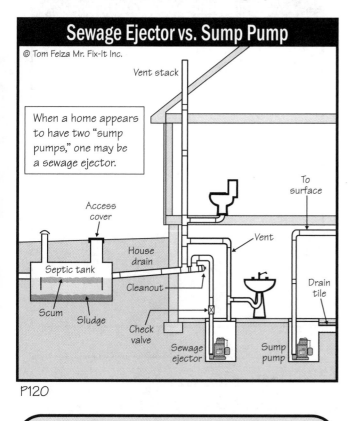

Sewage Ejector vs. Sump Pump

© Tom Feiza Mr. Fix-It Inc.

When a home appears to have two "sump pumps," one may be a sewage ejector.

Vent stack

Access cover

House drain

Septic tank

Cleanout

Scum

Sludge

Check valve

Sewage ejector

Sump pump

To surface

Vent

Drain tile

P120

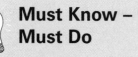

Must Know – Must Do

1. Understand the type of sewer systems in your home.

Plugged Drains

1. The most common reason for a slow drain is hair and other debris caught in the stopper assembly or trap.

2. Always try to remove the debris. Remove the stopper and try to catch the debris with a bent coat hanger or a special plastic tool with "hooks."

3. The next step would be to dismantle the trap. Try to avoid using chemicals.

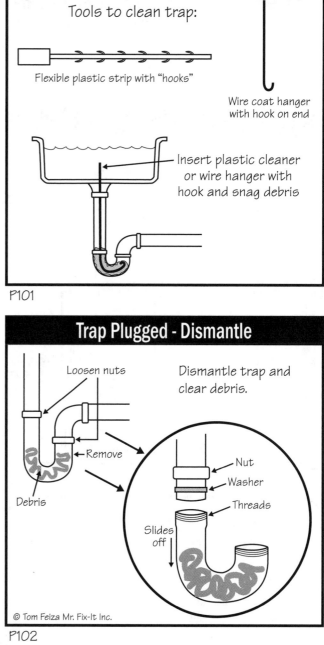

Trap Plugged - Clean with Wire or Tool

Tools to clean trap:

Flexible plastic strip with "hooks"

Wire coat hanger with hook on end

Insert plastic cleaner or wire hanger with hook and snag debris

P101

Trap Plugged - Dismantle

Loosen nuts

Dismantle trap and clear debris.

Remove

Debris

Nut

Washer

Threads

Slides off

© Tom Feiza Mr. Fix-It Inc.

P102

Chapter 10 – Electricity

Electrical – Overhead Feed

1. The main electrical feed to a home may be either overhead from a utility pole or underground.

2. The typical feed has three wires: two 120-volt wires and a neutral for 240-volt service.

3. Typical residential service provides 100 or 200 amps at 240 volts.

4. The utility company typically owns the feed wire up to your home.

5. For an overhead feed, wires will be more than 10 feet above the ground and must never extend over a swimming pool.

6. Modern systems will have a meter outside and an electrical breaker panel inside the home.

Electrical – Underground Feed

1. In newer construction, the electrical feed will be buried and then connected to a meter box outside the home.

2. The typical feed has three wires: two 120-volt wires and a neutral for 240-volt service.

3. Typical residential service provides 100 or 200 amps at 240 volts.

4. After the meter, the feed will connect to the main electrical service panel.

5. In a warm, dry climate, the main panel may be located outside.

6. For a cool, wet climate, the main panel will be located inside.

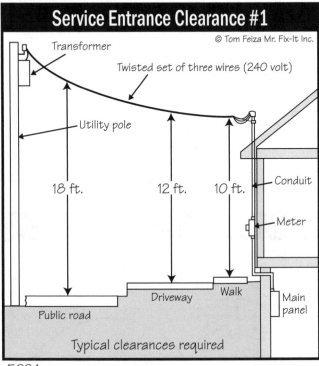

Service Entrance Clearance #1

© Tom Feiza Mr. Fix-It Inc.

Transformer

Twisted set of three wires (240 volt)

Utility pole

18 ft.　　12 ft.　　10 ft.

Conduit

Meter

Driveway　　Walk

Main panel

Public road

Typical clearances required

E024

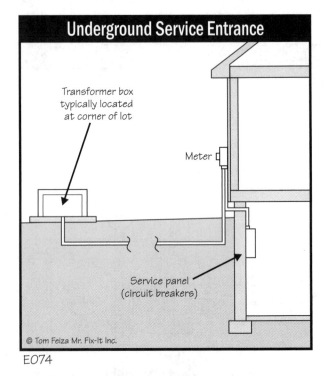

Underground Service Entrance

Transformer box typically located at corner of lot

Meter

Service panel (circuit breakers)

© Tom Feiza Mr. Fix-It Inc.

E074

Must Know – Must Do

1. Never disturb the overhead feed wires, meter or meter base.

2. Any work on this part of the system must be done by a professional.

Must Know – Must Do

1. Locate the main service panel and the main disconnect switch so you can turn off the power if necessary.

2. Never disturb the feed, meter or meter socket.

3. Any work on this part of the system must be done by a professional.

Electrical Main Panel

1. All power in a home is distributed through the main panel or circuit breaker panel.

2. On all modern systems, there will be one main 240-volt disconnect that turns off all power to the home.

3. Each large appliance will have its own circuit breaker, and 240-volt appliances will have a double breaker – that is, two 120-volt circuits.

4. Lighting and convenience outlets will be combined on several 120-volt breakers.

5. Terminology can be confusing. We may call a circuit 110- or 120-volt, and 220- or 240-volt.

6. The actual voltage on a 120-volt line will vary, depending on the utility service.

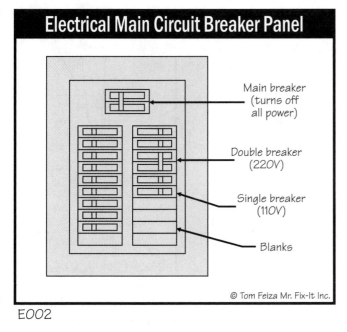

Electrical Main Circuit Breaker Panel

Main breaker (turns off all power)

Double breaker (220V)

Single breaker (110V)

Blanks

© Tom Feiza Mr. Fix-It Inc.

E002

Must Know – Must Do

1. Identify the main service disconnect and individual breakers.

2. Make sure everyone in the home knows how to turn off the main power.

Electrical Main Panel – Warm, Dry Climate

1. For a warm, dry climate, the main electrical panel may be located outside with the electrical meter.

2. On all modern systems, there will be one main 240-volt disconnect that turns off all power to the home.

3. Each large appliance will have its own circuit breaker, and 240-volt appliances will have a double breaker – that is, two 120-volt circuits.

4. Lighting and convenience outlets will be combined on several 120-volt breakers.

5. Terminology can be confusing. We may call a circuit 110- or 120-volt, and 220- or 240-volt.

6. The actual voltage on a 110- or 120-volt line will vary, depending on the utility service.

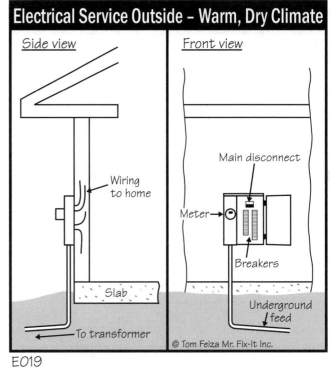

Electrical Service Outside – Warm, Dry Climate

Side view

Front view

Wiring to home

Main disconnect

Meter

Breakers

Slab

Underground feed

To transformer

© Tom Feiza Mr. Fix-It Inc.

E019

Must Know – Must Do

1. Identify the main service disconnect and individual breakers.

2. Make sure everyone in the home knows how to turn off the main power.

Ground Fault Circuit Interrupters (GFCI)

1. Your home should have a ground fault circuit interrupter (GFCI) protecting any outlet near a potential water or ground source – outlets in bathrooms and kitchens, those near sinks, and exterior or garage outlets.

2. The GFCI is a sensitive electrical switch that quickly stops the flow of electricity if there is a slight leakage to ground – or through your body.

3. The GFCI protects you from a shock.

4. A GFCI can be located in the main electrical panel as a special breaker with an extra button, or it may be part of a special electrical outlet with test and reset buttons.

5. Often, numerous outlets are protected by one GFCI.

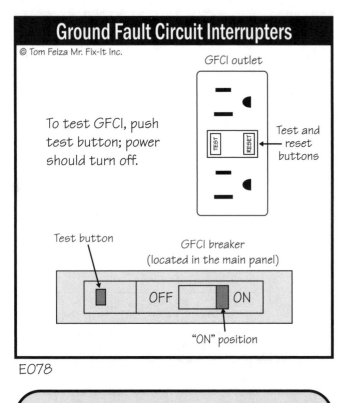

Ground Fault Circuit Interrupters

© Tom Feiza Mr. Fix-It Inc.

GFCI outlet

To test GFCI, push test button; power should turn off.

Test and reset buttons

TEST   RESET

Test button

GFCI breaker (located in the main panel)

OFF   ON

"ON" position

E078

Must Know – Must Do

1. Locate GFCIs and know what they control.
2. Test GFCIs monthly.

Polarity

1. Proper polarity is important because it protects you from a shocking experience.

2. Never modify the wiring to an outlet, fixture or cord.

3. Electricity flows like water – out the hot wire and back through the neutral wire.

4. You can receive a shock from either wire.

5. If a lamp has reversed polarity, it presents a shock hazard. You can receive a shock from the ring of the lamp socket, even when the switch and light are off.

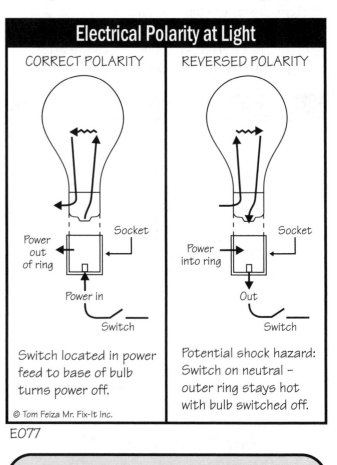

Electrical Polarity at Light

CORRECT POLARITY

REVERSED POLARITY

Power out of ring

Socket

Power in

Switch

Power into ring

Socket

Out

Switch

Switch located in power feed to base of bulb turns power off.

Potential shock hazard: Switch on neutral – outer ring stays hot with bulb switched off.

© Tom Feiza Mr. Fix-It Inc.

E077

Must Know – Must Do

1. Never do wiring unless you fully understand polarity and grounding.
2. Make sure all plugs and cords are original or installed by a professional.

Outlets, Cords and Plugs

1. The correct wiring of a cord and plug ensures that the electrical device is wired with correct polarity and grounding.

2. A grounded or three-prong plug provides an extra level of safety by providing a ground to the metal appliance.

3. Never modify a grounded plug. Limit the use of "cheater" plugs or adapters for a grounded appliance with a grounded plug.

4. A polarized plug has one wide blade and one narrow blade.

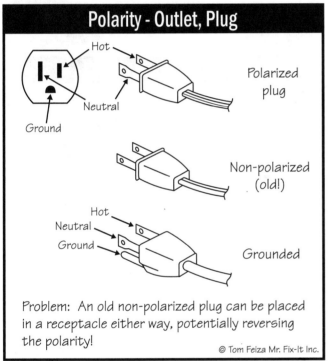

Polarity - Outlet, Plug

Hot

Polarized plug

Neutral

Ground

Non-polarized (old!)

Hot
Neutral
Ground

Grounded

Problem: An old non-polarized plug can be placed in a receptacle either way, potentially reversing the polarity!

© Tom Feiza Mr. Fix-It Inc.

E031

Must Know – Must Do

1. Never use a damaged plug or cord.

2. Never repair plugs, cords or outlets unless you understand polarity and grounding.

3. Avoid using adapters for grounded plugs and non-grounded outlets.

Circuit Breaker Resets

1. A circuit breaker will trip when there is an overload in the circuit.

2. When a breaker trips, the switch-like lever on the breaker will move from the on position to an off or tripped position.

3. Some breakers have a small window that shows a red flag when tripped.

4. Resetting some breakers require moving the lever to the full off position before moving to the on position.

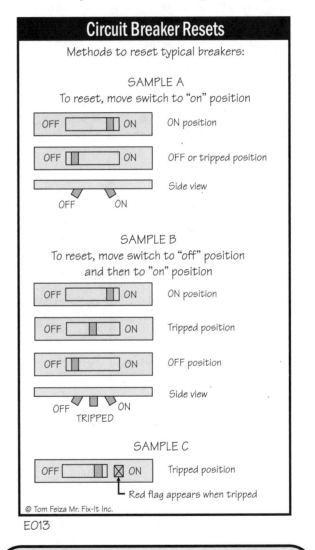

Circuit Breaker Resets

Methods to reset typical breakers:

SAMPLE A
To reset, move switch to "on" position

OFF [ON] — ON position

OFF [ON] — OFF or tripped position

OFF — ON — Side view

SAMPLE B
To reset, move switch to "off" position and then to "on" position

OFF [ON] — ON position

OFF [ON] — Tripped position

OFF [ON] — OFF position

OFF — TRIPPED — ON — Side view

SAMPLE C

OFF [⊠ ON] — Tripped position
└ Red flag appears when tripped

© Tom Feiza Mr. Fix-It Inc.

E013

Must Know – Must Do

1. Only reset a breaker if you know why the breaker tripped and after you have removed the excessive load.

2. If breaker trips several times, call a professional.

Carbon Monoxide

1. Carbon monoxide (CO) should be a concern for all homeowners because despite its danger, it has no taste, color or odor.

2. Many carbon monoxide problems are caused by poor maintenance or improper use of fuel-burning equipment.

3. Carbon monoxide is produced when fuel is burned, so any fuel-burning appliance is a potential source.

4. Proper maintenance and operation of fuel-burning equipment is essential.

5. Pay attention to gas furnaces and water heaters and their connections to chimneys.

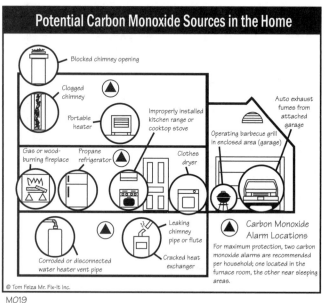

Potential Carbon Monoxide Sources in the Home

Blocked chimney opening
Clogged chimney
Portable heater
Improperly installed kitchen range or cooktop stove
Auto exhaust fumes from attached garage
Operating barbecue grill in enclosed area (garage)
Gas or wood-burning fireplace
Propane refrigerator
Clothes dryer
Leaking chimney pipe or flute
Corroded or disconnected water heater vent pipe
Cracked heat exchanger
Carbon Monoxide Alarm Locations
For maximum protection, two carbon monoxide alarms are recommended per household; one located in the furnace room, the other near sleeping areas.

© Tom Feiza Mr. Fix-It Inc.
M019

Must Know – Must Do

1. Use carbon monoxide alarms in your home, installed per instructions that came with the unit.

2. Maintain and understand all fuel-burning appliances.

3. Hire professionals for appliance service.

4. Never use a gasoline engine inside your home.

5. Never use a grill for heat inside your home.

Fire Safety

1. Contact your local fire department for fire safety information.

2. Always have modern smoke and fire detectors/alarms in your home.

3. Install and maintain smoke detectors per the manufacturer's instructions.

4. Replace the battery in each smoke detector as required.

5. Keep fire extinguishers in your home, and know how to use them.

6. Never store flammables in your home.

Smoke Detector / Alarm

Test once per month. Replace batteries yearly. Replace battery if "chirping." Replace unit before 10 years of age.

© Tom Feiza Mr. Fix-It Inc.
M011

Must Know – Must Do

1. Compile a list of emergency numbers. Post it for everyone in the home.

2. Establish an emergency escape plan, and practice it with your kids.

3. Test your smoke alarms; change batteries as needed.

4. Replace smoke alarms that are more than 10 years old.

5. Rely on local safety officials for specific local information.

Lead, Asbestos, Radon, Mold

1. **LEAD** – In homes built before 1978, there is a potential for lead in paint products. Lead can cause health problems if ingested. Lead-based paint in good condition usually doesn't present a problem, but peeling lead paint is hazardous. Lead paint used at windows creates health concerns because a window's movement can loosen paint. Check with local health officials or the Consumer Product Safety Commission on the proper maintenance and control of lead paint in your home.

2. **ASBESTOS** – Asbestos was used in building materials until the 1970s. The danger is that asbestos materials may become damaged and release asbestos fibers into the air. Studies have shown that people exposed to asbestos fibers have a higher risk of cancer and asbestosis. If you suspect you have asbestos materials in your home, have them evaluated by a professional. You can find more information through local health departments, the Consumer Product Safety Commission and the Environmental Protection Agency.

3. **RADON** – Radon is a naturally occurring radioactive gas that has been found in homes all over the U.S. Radon moves from the soil into our homes and can present a hazard at elevated levels. If you live in an area known for radon issues, have your home tested. You can obtain more information from local health officials and the Environmental Protection Agency.

4. **MOLD** – Mold has been around forever but has become a concern for homeowners since about 1990. The first defense is to keep materials in your home dry. Mold cannot survive without a water source. If you suspect you have a mold problem, contact your local or state health department.

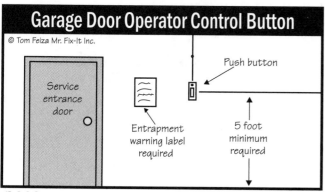

Garage Door Operator Control Button

© Tom Feiza Mr. Fix-It Inc.

Service entrance door

Push button

Entrapment warning label required

5 foot minimum required

D009

Electrical

1. Safety is very important when dealing with electricity. Always follow safety precautions and instructions for electrical devices.

2. Try to avoid using extension cords, and never run a cord through or across a doorway.

3. Always check the wattage rating for light fixtures. Never install a bulb that exceeds the rating (as shown in the illustration).

4. Incandescent bulbs create lots of heat and can be a fire hazard.

5. If you use an appliance with a grounded, three-prong plug, use a three-prong receptacle.

6. Avoid using an adapter for joining the three-prong plug to a two-prong outlet. If you must use an adapter, be sure to connect the grounding clip or wire.

7. Never use an extension cord that is frayed or has a damaged plug or insulation.

8. In locations near water, always install ground fault circuit interrupter outlets.

9. All permanently installed electrical equipment, such as the garage door operator and water softener, must be plugged directly into an electrical outlet.

10. Contact the Consumer Product Safety Commission for more electricity safety tips.

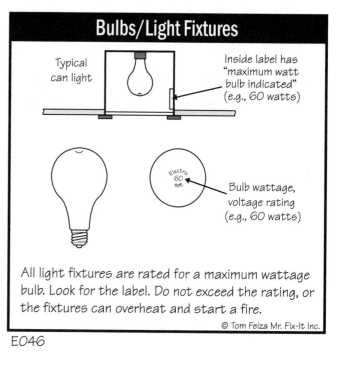

Bulbs/Light Fixtures

Typical can light

Inside label has "maximum watt bulb indicated" (e.g., 60 watts)

Electric 60 soft

Bulb wattage, voltage rating (e.g., 60 watts)

All light fixtures are rated for a maximum wattage bulb. Look for the label. Do not exceed the rating, or the fixtures can overheat and start a fire.

© Tom Feiza Mr. Fix-It Inc.

E046

Chapter 12 – Service Requirements

Service Requirements by the Calendar

Home operation and maintenance is easy if we understand our home systems and stay organized. A home operates just like a car – with the right maintenance, you can avoid major problems and efficiently run your home for many years. The key is preventing problems or catching small problems before they become home disasters.

If you don't change the filter on the furnace on a routine basis, you can freeze up the coil, and you will come home to a very warm house. If you don't turn off the exterior hose connection in the winter, you can come home to a flood.

This chapter provides that little bit of organization that helps us all remember to perform important preventive maintenance tasks. It offers lists of maintenance tasks to be performed on a routine basis. Refer to specific chapters in the book for detailed information on the specific tasks. Follow manufacturers' instructions for all service.

Remember, not every maintenance item will be applicable to your home or its systems. You need to do the homework here – study and understand the systems in your home.

Exercise caution before attempting inspection, maintenance or repairs. Turn off the power and disconnect other utility services. Follow any owner's manual supplied by the equipment manufacturer. If you don't understand a problem or system, consult a professional.

Daily and Weekly

Be aware of any changes or strange sounds in your home. If the automatic garage door opener is groaning, the door and track may need lubrication, or perhaps a roller is broken. If you smell sewer gas in the basement, it may be due to a dried-out floor drain trap. If the central air conditioner is squeaking, this may indicate a bad bearing on the fan motor. If a gutter is overflowing, expect water in the basement or crawl space. Just watch for changes, and address issues as they arise.

Be watchful during drastic weather changes. Weather can have a huge effect on our homes. A big snowstorm may make it necessary to clear your furnace's intake and discharge vent pipes. During periods of heavy rain, it is wise to check gutters and downspouts and make sure that the sump pump is working properly. If the furnace runs constantly or more often than you expect, check for a problem.

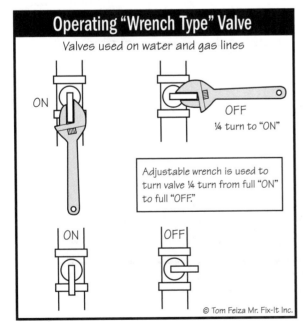

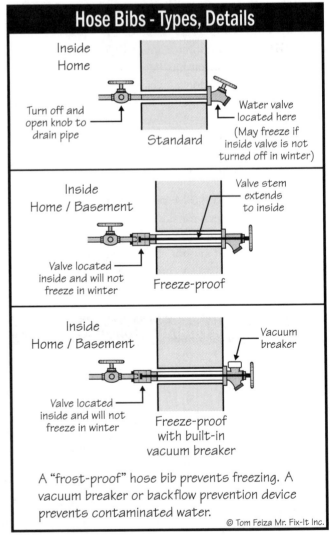

Monthly

When these systems are in use, perform the following checks monthly.

FIRE AND SMOKE ALARMS
Test alarm.

FIRE EXTINGUISHERS
Check pressure; service as needed.

CARBON MONOXIDE ALARM
Test alarm, and check reading.

WARM AIR HEATING SYSTEM
Check and change or wash filter (unless it's a special type).

FURNACE, HIGH EFFICIENCY
Check condensate drain to make sure it is clear and draining.

AIR CONDITIONING
Check and change or wash filter (unless it is a special type); check condensate drain to make sure it is clear and draining.

HEAT PUMP
Check and change or wash filter (unless it is a special type).

STEAM HEATING SYSTEM
Check water level. Service as needed.

SHOWER AND TUB DRAINS
Clear out hair and other debris.

GFCI
Test GFCI (ground fault circuit interrupter) outlets and breakers.

PLUMBING
Check for any leaks at fixtures, traps and piping.

WATER SOFTENER
Check salt supply.

CLOTHES DRYER
Clean lint from filter (after every use) and check duct for lint.

GARAGE DOOR OPERATOR
Test auto-reverse safety feature.

Spring

AIR CONDITIONING
Schedule professional service. Check that the unit is level and clean and has proper clearance. Adjust main duct dampers if needed.

HUMIDIFIER
Turn off unit and water supply. Switch humidifier's duct damper from winter to summer setting as needed.

DUCT DAMPERS
Adjust dampers for a switch from heating to cooling if necessary.

HIGH AND LOW RETURNS
Open high returns and close low returns for cooling season.

WHOLE HOUSE FAN
Check belt; lubricate and clean.

GUTTERS, DOWNSPOUTS
Clean gutters, and make sure downspouts are attached and extended.

ROOF
Inspect for damage. Trim trees if needed.

ROOF VENTS
Inspect for damage or bird nests.

CHIMNEY
Inspect for damage to cap, flashing and masonry.

SUMP PUMP
Test sump pump to make sure it removes water from the crock.

EXTERIOR, GENERAL
Check condition of paint, caulk and putty.

EXTERIOR, GROUNDS
Check that grading of soil and hard surfaces slopes away from the basement.

ATTIC
Check for signs of leaks, mildew, condensation.

BASEMENT
Check for signs of leaks, cracks, movement, rot, mildew.

CRAWL SPACE
Check for adequate ventilation to remove excess moisture.

DEHUMIDIFIER
Clean; start operation in basement as needed.

(Continued, next page)

Spring (continued)

PLUMBING
Open outside hose connection shutoff.

CLOTHES DRYER
Clean lint from duct and from unit per manufacturer's instructions.

REFRIGERATOR
Clean coil, clean drain pan, and check drain.

RANGE HOOD
Clean filter, wash fan blades.

BATHROOM EXHAUST FANS
Clean grill and fan.

BATHROOM TILE
Check grout, caulk and tile for damage.

WATER HEATER
Draw sediment from tank as needed.

SPRINKLERS, IRRIGATION
Service and start system.

DECKS
Clean and seal as needed.

Summer

AIR CONDITIONER
Keep bushes and plant material clear of unit. Maintain air conditioner's filter on furnace. Keep drain lines clear.

GUTTERS, DOWNSPOUTS
Clean gutters, and make sure downspouts are attached and extended.

SUMP PUMP
Test sump pump to make sure it removes water from the crock.

EXTERIOR
Complete any major paint, putty, wood repair and caulking projects.

FIREPLACE
Schedule professional cleaning and service as needed.

WOOD STOVES
Schedule professional cleaning and service.

CHIMNEY AND ROOF
Schedule professional service as needed.

EXTERIOR METAL
Check metal railings. Paint as needed.

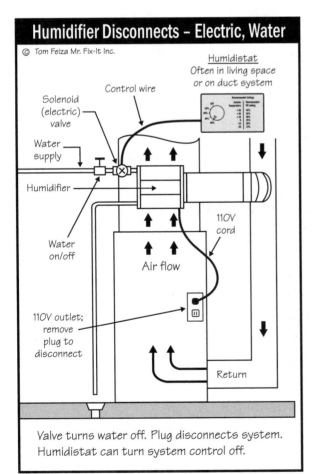

Humidifier Disconnects – Electric, Water

© Tom Feiza Mr. Fix-It Inc.

Humidistat
Often in living space or on duct system

Control wire

Solenoid (electric) valve

Water supply

Humidifier

Water on/off

Air flow

110V cord

110V outlet; remove plug to disconnect

Return

Valve turns water off. Plug disconnects system. Humidistat can turn system control off.

E064

AC Condenser – Clearance to Vents

Air flow

Direct vent water heater exhaust

Dryer vent

A/C

Lint

House vents should not be near the AC compressor or condenser. Clothes dryer lint can quickly plug coils. Combustion products can damage the coils.

© Tom Feiza Mr. Fix-It Inc.

A036

Fall

AIR CONDITIONING
Cover top of unit if desired at end of cooling season.

HEATING
Schedule professional service; lubricate fan, motor, and pumps.

OIL HEAT
Arrange for maintenance and oil delivery.

WATER HEATER
Service gas and oil water heaters. Draw sediment from tank as needed. Check for carbon monoxide.

HUMIDIFIER
Service, clean, and change water panel as needed. Switch duct damper as needed from summer to winter setting.

DUCT DAMPERS
Adjust dampers for the switch from cooling to heating if necessary.

HIGH AND LOW RETURNS
Open low returns and close high returns for heating season.

GUTTERS, DOWNSPOUTS
Clean gutters, and make sure downspouts are attached and extended.

ROOF
Inspect for damage; trim trees as needed.

ROOF VENTS
Inspect for damage or bird nests.

CHIMNEY
Inspect for damage to cap, flashing and masonry.

SUMP PUMP
Test sump pump to make sure it removes water from the crock.

EXTERIOR, GENERAL
Check condition of paint, caulk and putty.

WEATHERSTRIPPING
Check and repair weatherstripping on windows and doors.

EXTERIOR, GROUNDS
Check that grading of soil and hard surfaces slopes away from basement.

BASEMENT
Check for any signs of leaks, cracks, movement, rot, mildew.

CRAWL SPACE
Check for adequate ventilation to remove excess moisture.

PLUMBING
Close outside hose connection shutoff.

CLOTHES DRYER
Clean lint from duct and unit per manufacturer's instructions.

BATHROOM TILE
Check grout, caulk and tile for damage.

GARAGE DOOR
Tighten all hardware, and lubricate moving parts.

FIREPLACE
Check flue, damper, firebox.

SPRINKLERS, IRRIGATION
Drain and service system.

ROOM AIR CONDITIONER
Remove unit, or install cover.

SWIMMING POOL
Service and close.

HOSES
Remove from hose bibs; drain to prevent freezing.

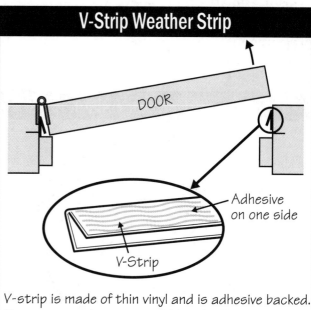

V-Strip Weather Strip

DOOR

Adhesive on one side

V-Strip

V-strip is made of thin vinyl and is adhesive backed. To use, cut with scissors, fold and adhere with adhesive strip. Excellent for windows and doors with a tight fit.

© Tom Feiza Mr. Fix-It Inc.

D006

Winter

FIRE AND SMOKE ALARMS
Change batteries, vacuum to remove dust, and test.

CARBON MONOXIDE ALARMS
Change batteries, and test.

ROOF AND GUTTERS
Monitor for ice dams, and record problems for future corrective work.

SUMP PUMP
Test sump pump to make sure it removes water from the crock.

FURNACE
Lubricate fan, motor, and pumps as required at mid-season.

WASHING MACHINE
Check supply hoses for damage. Clean screens in hose connections.

DOORS AND HARDWARE
Lubricate hinges and moving parts.

BOILER
Lubricate pump twice per year.

STEAM BOILER
Check water level.

GUTTERS
Keep downspouts extended.

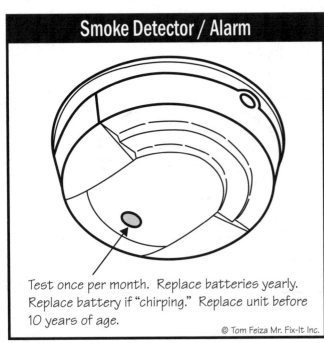

Smoke Detector / Alarm

Test once per month. Replace batteries yearly. Replace battery if "chirping." Replace unit before 10 years of age.

© Tom Feiza Mr. Fix-It Inc.

MO11

Periodic Maintenance and Service as Needed

SEPTIC SYSTEM
Schedule professional pumping and inspection at least every two years.

WATER SOFTENER
Clean brine tank and screens or filters as needed.

WELL SYSTEM
Test water for bacteria and other contaminants. Check pressure tank operation.

FIRE AND SMOKE ALARMS
Replace alarms every 10 years.

FIREPLACE
Schedule cleaning and inspection as needed, depending on use.

WATER FILTERS
Replace as needed.

ELECTRIC BASEBOARD
Vacuum and clean based on usage.

GAS APPLIANCES
Check flexible gas connectors for stove, dryer, etc., yearly.

RANGE HOOD
Clean filter and fan.

SHUTOFFS
Periodically review all utility disconnects with your family.

TERMITES AND OTHER PESTS
Schedule professional inspections and service as needed.

ELECTRICAL
Eliminate extension cords. Check for damaged cords, plugs or outlets.

WATER HEATER
Test temperature and pressure relief valve. Replace leaking valves.

PLUMBING
Test main water shutoff. If it is hard to operate, call a plumber.

HOW TO OPERATE YOUR HOME – Product Catalog

Products are available through book retailers, from Internet bookstores, and directly from our offices.
Wholesale discounts are available for quantity purchases through How to Operate Your Home.

HOW TO OPERATE YOUR HOME
Professional Edition

(ISBN 978-0-9832018-2-3) $29.95

The ultimate guide for operating your home – just like an owner's manual for your car. Answers all those questions about how a home works and how you should be operating your home. Full-color cover, 304 pages, over 600 illustrations.

MY HOME – MI CASA
Tips To Operate Your Home in Spanish/English

(ISBN 978-0-9674759-6-7) $19.95

Spanish and English guide to all systems in your home. Over 300 illustrations in Spanish and English. Operate, maintain, and repair your home. Full-color cover, 160 pages.

HOW TO OPERATE YOUR HOME
Standard Edition

(ISBN 978-0-9832018-3-0) $18.95

A 160-page "systems only" version of How To Operate Your Home with a full-color cover and over 300 illustrations. Includes the first eight chapters of How To Operate Your Home plus a bonus chapter on emergency shutoffs.

MY HOME
Tips for Operating Your Home

(ISBN 978-0-9832018-4-7) $14.95

A quick guide to help you operate your home. Over 150 illustrations and explanations of how systems work. Full-color cover, 64 pages.

HOW TO OPERATE YOUR HOME
Basic Edition

$14.95

A guide to most basic systems found in homes. Designed as a cost-effective attachment to your home inspection report, and three-hole-drilled for easy addition to a binder.

HOME SYSTEMS ILLUSTRATED

(ISBN 978-0-9832018-6-1) $295.95

Over 1,500 line art images, 250 color illustrations, and 150 Spanish images of home systems, equipment, construction details, operational tips, typical problems and more. Illustrations are provided in JPG format on a CD/download. The 360-page reference book displays all illustrations.

MR. FIX-IT QUICK TIPS

$275 for 13 Tips

Do you want to keep in touch with your customers but lack the content? Let Quick Tips do the talking for you. Send as e-mails (including Constant Contact®), use in newsletters and other printed material, and publish on your website. 26 new tips every year. Unlimited use.

HOME TIPS

$89 for 10 articles

10 Mr. Fix-It Home Tips PDF articles for your website, email, printing, and newsletters. Typical topics: Keep Your Basement Dry, Window Condensation, Replace Your Roof. Delivered electronically. 65 pages full of content.

Custom printing is available for large orders.

Visit **www.htoyh.com** or **www.HowToOperateYourHome.com** for information on all our products, or to order online.

Quantity discounts are available for large orders.
Contact How to Operate Your Home – 262-303-4884, mail@htoyh.com

HOW TO OPERATE YOUR HOME

Notes